A Dime's Difference?

Democrats, Republicans, and the US National Debt

Charles F. Stamper

www.breathittpublishing.com

ISBN: 146378208X
ISBN-13: 978-1463782085

For Celestine Stamper

"A wife of noble character is her husband's crown"

Proverbs 12:4

For Emma-Grace Diane Stamper

Jesus said, "Let the little children come to me, and do not hinder them, for the kingdom of heaven belongs to such as these"

Matthew 19:14

CONTENTS

PROLOGUE

In the summer of 2008 a one term sitting Senator from Illinois, a Democrat, Barack Obama, was locked in a typically nasty campaign for the office of President of the United States of America with the four term sitting Senator from Arizona, a Republican, John McCain. The Vice-Presidential candidates were Joseph Biden, a sitting six term Senator from Delaware, and Sarah Palin, sitting Governor of Alaska, respectively.

As has become normal in American politics, more likely it has always been the case and I just chose this moment in time to notice it, there were a lot of speeches, statements, interviews, sound bites, and the like from both parties that just did not seem completely accurate even upon first listening by a person of largely superficial first hand knowledge of the issues. I'm sure you have already guessed, that person of largely superficial first hand knowledge of the issues was me.

In the fall of 2007 my wife and I were blessed with the arrival of our first, and to date only, child. This beautiful little girl named Emma-Grace had engendered in me an increased sense of responsibility for, well just about everything under the sun. I am certain that any of you that have children can relate to this feeling. I was then, and still am today, determined to make the best decisions that I possibly can in order to provide her every opportunity for success and happiness. Therefore, I decided that I should become much better informed on political issues with the expectation that this would inform my choices about not only candidates and parties, but also about accurate sources of information from the world of "media", whether old, new, newspaper, television, radio, books, magazines, internet, or any other method known or unknown. The period of study that followed has been illuminating to say the least, depressing, frustrating, infuriating, etc. etc., to say a little more.

If you have ever listened to Sean Hannity, Rush Limbaugh, watched Fox News, read Ann Coulter, or Mark Levin, among others, you have certainly heard of the "liberal" bias of the so called main stream media. Well, much to my chagrin, I now believe this liberal bias undeniably exists. Score one for the conservatives. On the other side of things the likes of Chris Matthews, Keith Olbermann, CNN, Michael Moore, among others, will tell you all about the "vast right wing conspiracy", Well, much to my chagrin, I now believe this "vast right wing conspiracy" undeniably exists. Score one for the liberals, and we are now tied at 1 all. Depressing, demoralizing, I can't really think of any more words that begin with de-, but I think you get the point.

Of the many things that have emerged from this effort is a newly registered independent voter. I have become so disillusioned by what I have been finding that I, a lifelong Democrat, have changed my voter registration. I am actually an "other" as in my home state of Kentucky the form lists only Democrat, Republican, or Other. A second, is a new career for me. The first product of that new career is the book you now hold in your hands. This book, as will be the case with anything coming from my desk, is an effort to provide some factual information on the topic(s) under consideration. I hope you find it interesting, useful, and even a little entertaining. Trust me, if you are going to become more actively involved in the governance of your nation, and it so very desperately needs for you to do just that, you are going to need a very well exercised sense of humor.

After realizing that the sun was still rising every morning and setting every evening, I decided that I could get up and go on with life. But to what end? Was I to just throw up my hands and allow what will happen to happen with no attempt to do anything. Just hope and pray for something better for my wife, daughter, family, and friends. No, not any longer. We can improve our situation. We can move our society to a better place. I believe that it is fair to consider a government, any government, a reflection of its citizenry. I further believe that all legitimate authority to govern comes from the consent of those governed. Therefore, it seems clear that the ultimate responsibility for the results of our government, both good and bad, rests with each of us.

So, in the interest of full disclosure I have seen this quote, or variations on the theme, attributed to many different authors, including President Reagan. I will leave it as anonymous. It is in this spirit we go forward.

"If not us, who? If not now, when?"

Charles F. Stamper

Georgetown, KY Summer 2011

1 - BEGINNING AT THE BEGINNING

"I don't make things complicated, they just get that way, all by themselves"

Martin Riggs

Lethal Weapon

"In the beginning God created the heavens and the earth. Now the earth was formless and empty, darkness was over the surface of the deep and the Spirit of God was hovering over the waters."

Okay, perhaps that is a little too far back for the purposes of this book. However, it does illustrate the question, and the complexities that arise when considering even the seemingly simplest of them. What is the beginning of the United States of America? In the spirit of, he who writes the book gets to make the decisions, here goes.

On 5 September, 1774, at Carpenter's Hall in Philadelphia, Pennsylvania, a convention of delegates representing 12 of the 13 colonies met in what has become known as the First Continental Congress. This Congress was attended by 56 members who had been appointed by the legislatures of their colonies, the exception being Georgia which was not represented. The Congress was called in response to the passage of "Intolerable Acts" by the British Parliament. Among several other things, this Congress petitioned King George III for redress of colonial grievances, and additionally called for another Continental Congress in the event that their petition was unsuccessful in halting enforcement of the "Intolerable Acts".

As I am sure you have gathered by the fact that this book has not ended, no acceptable redress was forthcoming from King George III. In fact, in May of 1775 British General Thomas Gage, Gage had been installed as governor of Massachusetts when the British removed their right of self governance in response to the Boston Tea Party, sent out a column of British troops to seize rebel arms. The column was confronted by local militia, or minutemen, and the Battles of Lexington and Concord ensued.

On 10 May, 1775, the Second Continental Congress, this time with delegates from all 13 colonies began meeting in Philadelphia. This second Congress acted as the de facto national government of what was to become the United States of America. This Congress raised armies, directed strategy, appointed diplomats, made formal treaties, and managed the colonial war effort. On 11 June, 1776 a committee was appointed to prepare a draft of The United States Declaration of Independence which was adopted on 4 July, 1776. This day is celebrated annually as American Independence Day.

On 12 June, 1776 the Congress resolved to appoint a committee of 13 to prepare a draft of a constitution for a union of states. A final draft of the document, which was to be known as the Articles of Confederation, was approved for ratification of the states on 15 November 1777. This final draft of the Articles served as the de facto system of government used by the Congress, "the United States in Congress Assembled", until ratification on 1 March, 1781, at which point the Second Continental Congress become known as the Congress of the Confederation.

There was now a government of the United States of America capable of making war, negotiating diplomatic agreements, and borrowing money. The articles did not, however, provide for a President, nor any executive agencies, nor a judiciary, and no tax base.

Lacking authority to levy taxes the Congress of the Confederation could instead, request the states to contribute money to the common treasury. However, it could not punish a state for not contributing its share for the federal budget. Control of taxation and tariffs was left to the states, and each state could issue its own currency. In disputes between states, and quarrels over state boundaries, the Congress of the Confederation played the role of mediator and judge but could not require states to accept its decisions. Without the power to collect taxes, the federal government plunged into debt.

By June, 1784, Virginia recognized the need for an agreement with Maryland respecting the navigation and jurisdiction of the Potomac River, and appointed a commission of four to "frame such liberal and equitable regulations concerning the said river as may be mutually advantageous to the two States". January, 1785, Maryland responds to the Virginia resolution by appointing a like number of commissioners for the purpose of "settling the navigation and jurisdiction over that part of the bay of Chesapeake which lies within the limits of Virginia, and over the rivers Potomac and Pocomoke with full power on behalf of Maryland to adjudge and settle the jurisdiction to be exercised by the said State, respectively, over the waters and navigation of the same."

In March, 1785, the two commissions meet at the Mount Vernon, home of George Washington, during which time they drafted a compact which, in many of its details relative to the navigation and jurisdiction of the Potomac, is still in force to this day. More importantly, the commissioners submitted to their respective states a report in favor of a convention of all the states "to take into consideration the trade and commerce" of the Confederation.

Annapolis was accepted as the place, and the first Monday in September 1786 as the time, for the convention. The attendance at Annapolis proved disappointing. Only five States were represented. Because of the small representation, the Annapolis Convention did not deem it "advisable to proceed on the business of their mission." After an exchange of views, the Annapolis delegates unanimously submitted to their respective States a report in which they suggested that a convention of representatives from all the States meet at Philadelphia on 13 May 1787 to examine the defects in the existing system of government and formulate "a plan for supplying such defects as may be discovered".

On 21 February 1787, the Congress of the Confederation resolved: "It is expedient that on the second Monday in May next a Convention of delegates who shall have been appointed by the several States be held at Philadelphia for the sole and express purpose of revising the Articles of Confederation."

25 May 1787 the Constitutional Convention began its deliberations. The delegates labored throughout the summer and into the fall, resolving issues large and small, up to and including the Great Compromise which resolved the issue of the number of representatives each state would have. On 8 September 1787, a committee of five, William Samuel Johnson of Connecticut, Alexander Hamilton of New York, Gouverneur Morris of Pennsylvania, James Madison of Virginia, and Rufus King of Massachusetts. was appointed "to revise the style of and arrange the articles which had been agreed to by the House."

The Convention met on Monday, 17 September, for its final session. Several of the delegates were disappointed in the result. Some delegates left before the ceremony, and three of those remaining refused to sign, Edmund Randolph and George Mason of Virginia, and Elbridge Gerry of Massachusetts. Of the thirty-nine who did sign, their views were ably summed up by Benjamin Franklin, who said, "There are several parts of this Constitution which I do not at present approve, but I am not sure I shall never approve them." He would accept the Constitution, however, "because I expect no better and because I am not sure that it is not the best."

On 7 December 1787, Delaware became the first State to ratify the new Constitution, with its vote being unanimous. Pennsylvania ratified on 12 December 1787, by a vote of 46 to 23 (66.67%). New Jersey ratified on 19 December 1787, and Georgia on 2 January 1788, both with unanimous votes. The requirement of ratification by nine states, set by Article Seven of the Constitution, was met when New Hampshire voted to ratify, on 21 June 1788.

On 30 April 1789, George Washington was inaugurated and the first presidential term began. The first United States Congress had begun meeting on 4 March 1789 and the organizing of a new government, our second form of government both being known as The United States of America, began. For the purposes of this book, and in the authors opinion, the technical beginning of the present day United States of America was 21 June 1788.

As for our financial history, the first fiscal year for The United States of America was 1 January 1789. Congress changed the beginning of the fiscal year from 1 January to 1 July in 1842, and finally from 1 July to 1 October in 1977 where it remains today. The most reliable data I can find on the national debt under our second and current government, if you consider the federal government reliable, is 1 January 1791 at which time our national debt was $75,463,476.52.

That, ladies and gentlemen, is the end of the beginning, or as some might say, the beginning of the end.

Remember, "I don't make things complicated, they just get that way, all by themselves".

Charles F. Stamper

2 - OF DEBT AND DEFICITS

"It is the set of the sails, not the direction of the wind that determines which way we will go. "

Jim Rohn

What, exactly, is the national debt? What, exactly, is the budget deficit? Questions that seem fairly straight forward, after all nearly all of us have a mortgage or know someone who does, or a car payment, or credit card payments, or student loan payments, or or or or or.... and therefore have a grasp on what debt is, even if we haven't thought about it in terms of deficits and surpluses. But, as with most things related to our government, it isn't quite as simple as it seems, or as it should be.

In keeping with chapter 1 we will begin at the beginning, and start off with a simple example. Lets look at a vastly simplified household budget. Lets say you just graduated and got a great shiny new job, or maybe wrote a book that sold fabulously well, who knew grandma had money to buy that many copies? Your shiny new job, or book as it may be, is paying you, as in take home pay (net), $60,000.00 per year. Remember, I told you this was vastly simplified, we don't pay taxes or anything inconvenient like that. Now I know you have to make a lot more money than that to avoid taxes for real, but just play along with me here.

Of course we all know that a year begins on 1 January and ends on 31 December. Well someone, somewhere, at sometime decided that was just to complicated for financial purposes, and so, we have something called a fiscal year. Fiscal years may be user defined and our Congress has changed the federal fiscal year on multiple occasions. The first fiscal year for the Constitutional United States Government, as opposed to the United States Government chartered by the Articles of Confederation, was on 1 January, 1789. Congress changed the beginning of the fiscal year from 1 January to 1 July in 1842, and finally from 1 July to 1 October in 1977 where it remains today. For the duration of this little example we are going to use the calendar year as our fiscal year.

For that first year, you are content to live in Mom and Dad's basement, drive your trusty old rust bucket of a car, and generally scrimp and save until finally on 31 December you tally up how much you have made and subtract out how much you have spent. At the end of this little exercise you discover that you have managed to save $20,000.00 over the course of this your first fiscal year. Congratulations are definitely in order. You have just done something that the federal government has only managed 12 times since 1940, and that is to finish a fiscal year with a surplus. Meaning (your income – your expenses) resulted in a positive number. In your case a $20,000.00 positive number, or surplus.

The very next day, 1 January of year 2, you are telling Mom and Dad all about your accomplishment over the past year, and while very proud, Mom and Dad decide that you are perfectly capable of doing your own laundry, cooking your own meals, and the like, therefore Mom isn't going to do any of the above anymore. On top of that Dad said something about RENT!!! Looks like living in the basement may not be the best life plan after all. A couple of weeks or months go by, who can keep track. While watching a Pinky and the Brain marathon, and mulling over your life situation, you happen to see a commercial with this cool hot air balloon and notice they are talking about real estate. You, yes you, can own your own home with little or no money down! That's it! You need to buy your own home. The search is on.

After an exhausting search on the web site of this real estate company, which lasted tens of minutes, maybe even an hour, you find your perfect starter home across town. You send an inquiry by email, and the next day a very friendly real estate agent calls you up and sets an appointment for you to view the property. The day of the appointment comes, you love everything about the house and the neighborhood, you also learn that the house will cost you $100,000.00. You suddenly realize that the math doesn't work out, you only have $20,000.00 in savings, and with Dad charging you rent that number isn't going to rise very quickly. No need to fret, remember that very friendly real estate agent, well at this point they will probably introduce you to an equally friendly banker who will in turn introduce you to our first debt instrument, the good old mortgage. By the way did you know that the word *mortgage* literally means 'dead pledge'. It comes from Old French *mortgage*, and is a compound formed from *mort* 'dead' and *gage* 'pledge', but I digress.

So, you meet with the banker and he/she explains that you can use your $20,000.00 as a down payment and the bank, in return for your promise to repay, over time, principal plus interest, will loan you the remaining $80,000.00. The written version of your promise to repay with all of the terms and conditions, interest rates, repayment time horizon, and the like is called a mortgage.

Time goes by, you get moved into your new home and before you know it, it is 31 December of year two and you sit down and look at your books again. Remember your first fiscal year you achieved a surplus of $20,000.00. Well in year two you purchased your own home with that $20,000.00 and an $80,000.00 mortgage. You were not able to save any money at all for the balance of year two, with moving expenses and buying assorted furnishings and the like. Welcome to the land of deficits, the amount you earn − the amount you spend = negative number, (you earned $60,000.00 + your $20,000.00 in savings) − (you spent your $60,000.00 income on expenses + $20,000.00 savings on down payment + $80,000.00 in mortgage debt). All of that adds up to -$80,000.00. You ran an $80,000.00 dollar budget deficit in your second fiscal year.

The next day is 1 January, or the first day of your third fiscal year. Now your budget forms get just a little more complicated. Your mortgage payment is a new line item under your expenses, and there is a totally new column entitled debt. This is where the $80,000.00 will be reflected. Now we will fast forward to 31 December of year 3 and look at our books once more. You took a Dave Ramsey class this past year and learned how to live on your $60,000.00 dollar income. Lets say that your monthly expenses averaged $4,000.00, this amount multiplied by 12 months comes to $48,000.00. Welcome back to the land of surpluses, Income or $60,000.00 – expenses or $48,000.00 = a positive $12,000.00. Let's also assume that your monthly mortgage payment was $1,000.00 and that exactly half of that went to principal and the other half to interest. When you begin your budget forms for your fourth year, your savings column comes back to life with $12,000.00 dollars in it, and your debt column will be decreased by the amount of principal you paid or $6,000.00, so it will drop to $74,000.00.

Now this was all, very obviously, vastly simplified, but basically this represents a budget. It should list all of the monies that come in and it should also list all of the monies going out. So long as this basic rule is followed you now have a dependably accurate document to help you analyze your spending habits and stay on track to accomplish your financial goals whatever they may be. Remember earlier I said that most things with the government aren't quite as simple as they seem, or should be? Well here is a perfect case in point. Our government has decided that some items are to be "off" budget.

A relatively recent example of this would be the fact that the administration of President George W. Bush decided that the cost of the wars in Iraq and Afghanistan should be "off" budget. So what is the big deal you say? Well first things first, the deficits that were projected and then reported by the administration were grossly understated, resulting in the national debt growing much, much faster that the accumulated deficits would suggest. Keep in mind, just because you choose not to report money you have spent on your budget, does not mean it will not follow you. To go back to our example, how different would your budget have looked had you chosen to place your mortgage "off" budget? However, the bank to whom you owe the money will still come after you for it whether you report it on your budget or not. So in reality all you are doing is lying to yourself or possibly your spouse, or the voting public.

There you have it, in its absolutely simplest terms. When you boil it all down and strip away all of the devices and language designed to confuse, complicate, and distract. It is simply a matter of how much you take in minus how much you spend. No matter if your talking about your household, the company you work for, or the nation of which you call yourself a citizen.

Keep in mind that I am neither an accountant nor an economist. I am just an everyday guy, educated in the public school system, who, remarkable though it may be, somehow learned to read and comprehend. All that was missing was taking the time to do the research for myself. Well I have now done that research and you are holding it in your hands.

I have always wanted to write a book in which I would be able to say this!

"The author of this book is not engaged in rendering legal, accounting, or other professional advice. Since your situation is fact dependent, you should also seek the counsel of a competent professional."

Back to the business at hand, it's time to take a look at each of our administrations, and the condition of our nations finances, as measured by the national debt. This rather narrow focus was picked quite on purpose. All to often, in the political climate we find ourselves in, any discussion quickly devolves into shouting matches of people attempting to rationalize the results of those they support while demonizing the results of those they oppose. This book and its author are willing to stipulate that all Presidents and all administrations have faced, or are facing, their own unique set of challenges and opportunities. With that in mind I wanted to set a standard that was as objective as possible against which to measure our administrations through history. So we will strip away all of the extenuating circumstances and ask the following question of each administration:

"How was your financial stewardship of the United States of America?"

Hopefully, we can encourage some rational discussion based on logic and thought, to at least accompany the emotional histrionics pervade by both sides in our current political discourse. With a little luck we may be able to determine the direction in which we are traveling, and perhaps even who set the sails.

Charles F. Stamper

3 - 1789 – 1869
(PRESIDENTS 1 THROUGH 20 &
CONGRESSES 1 THROUGH 40)

"Be kind and considerate with your criticism... It's just as hard to write a bad book as it is to write a good book."

Malcolm Cowley

First off, I think I should probably warn you that we are going to be using some words throughout the remainder of this book whose definitions have been obfuscated by those that pass themselves off as politicians, political thinkers, reporters and the like here in the early 21st century United States. Be advised, some readers may find these words objectionable and even disturbing, you are advised to avert your eyes and skip down to the next line as we have taken extreme care not to place any such words close to one another. Alternatively, you could consider the purchase of a dictionary. Please consider this your parental warning.

I know what your thinking, obfuscated is a good word and it is, but it is not one of those being referred to here. By the way, some of the following text is a bit of a review of previous chapters included here so you don't have to flip back to refresh your memory, and yes your most welcome. You see, one of the more compelling **"facts"** (there is the first potentially disturbing word) in this book, and one you will probably never hear anywhere else, is this. This nation was born deeply in debt. It is not a new phenomenon, and this isn't even the first time this nation has teetered on the brink of financial collapse. We as a nation borrowed what was, at the time, massive sums of money to fund the fighting of the revolutionary war. Our first form of federal government was based upon the Articles of Confederation and consisted of the Confederation Congress. This Confederation Congress was the sum total of the federal government, as the Articles did not provide for a judicial nor a executive branch of the federal government, and had left the fledgling new nation in such desperate financial straights as to engender the calling of a Constitutional Convention to repair defects in the Articles of Confederation a scant 11 years after the signing of The Declaration of Independence.

This Convention would eventually produce what we now know as The Constitution of the United States of America and, after being ratified by at least 9 of the 13 original colonies, would replace the Articles of Confederation as the supreme law of the land. On 21 June 1788, New Hampshire became that 9th state to ratify. Virginia followed on 25 June 1788, and then New York as number 11 on 26 July 1788. At this point the wheels were set in motion and on 4 March 1789 the 1st United States Congress, consisting of the United States Senate and the United States House of Representatives, met at Federal Hall at 26 Wall Street, in New York. Soon there after, on 30 April 1789, George Washington was inaugurated as the first President of The United States of America, once again in the City of New York. Thus began the formation of the second, first constitutionally based and still current, form of government for our nation. Upon formation, the Constitutional government assumed the debts that had been incurred under the Confederation Congress, as well as those debts which had been assumed by each of the individual states. Although the new government was formed in 1789 the first fiscal year for the United States is defined as 01 January 1791, resulting in that first fiscal year actually being 1 year and 8 months in length, at which time the total national debt was $75,463,476.52.

The length of both Presidential and Vice-Presidential terms is set to four years in Article II Section 1 of the Constitution, while Article I Section 2 defines the term of the members of the House of Representatives at two years to be chosen in full every two years, and finally, Article I Section 3 sets the term of a Senator to 6 years with 1/3 to be elected every second year. We will be looking at each administration as opposed to each President and the 2 corresponding Congresses at a time. For example the first administration of President George Washington was from 30 April 1789 through 3 March 1793 and encompassed both the first and the second Congresses. With the first United States Congress running from 4 March 1789 through 3 March 1791, and the second running from 4 March 1791 through 3 March 1793.

One of the objectives for this book is to be an enjoyable read, if that's possible given all the dates, names, and numbers that the topic entails. To that end we have come up with a format that I hope accomplishes this goal. Beginning on the very next page you will find a brief summary of each administration, and the 2 corresponding Congresses. In keeping with the, strip away all extenuating circumstances theme, there will be very little in the way of significant political events found here, although we will pass on some hopefully interesting, even if pretty much useless, bits of information from the period and occasionally the personalities under review.

This chapter contains Presidents 1 through 19, chapter 4 contains 20 through 38 and both will follow this format. Beginning with chapter 5, we will expand our discussion a bit dedicating a chapter each to the remaining Presidents. All the while we will keep a running count of those administrations that increased the debt and those that reduced it. Yes, we have actually had administrations pay down the debt. For those of you who happen to have been born in the year this last happened, happy 83rd birthday to you!

Now that the stage has been set, we will begin our examination of the national debt of the United States, and the role each of our administrations and Congresses have played in it's development throughout the years. At the end we hope to have a objective tally allowing us to compare our 2 major political parties, and their respective claim on the legacy of responsible financial stewardship. So take a little break, get your favorite drink, have a seat in your favorite chair and when you get back we will get started.

While you're gone we will pretend the music from Jeopardy is playing....

the music ends.
Welcome back, lets get back at it.

George Washington was inaugurated as our first President in New York City on 30 April 1789. At the time of the inauguration political parties as we know them simply didn't exist. There were however, factions, that would organize for limited amounts of time, typically in support of a single issue. The first real political party was the Federalist organized by Alexander Hamilton in 1791. In response, Thomas Jefferson organized the Democratic-Republican party a year later. In broad strokes the Federalist were in support of a stronger federal government, stronger even than that outlined in the Constitution, while the Democratic-Republican's were in favor of protecting state sovereignty. By the way, does anyone else find it ironic that one of our very first political parties was named the Democratic-Republicans, I'm just saying.

These events were likely instrumental in George Washington's decision to seek and serve a second term as President. He made his opinion of political parties clear in an open letter to the people of the United States, which is better known as his farewell address. In it he said the following:

"However combinations or associations of the above description may now and then answer popular ends, they are likely, in the course of time and things, to become potent engines, by which cunning, ambitious, and unprincipled men will be enabled to subvert the power of the people and to usurp for themselves the reins of government, destroying afterwards the very engines which have lifted them to unjust dominion."

The entire text of this address can be found in appendix 2 at the back of this book.

Most often you will see President Washington identified as a Federalist, and given his support of the Constitution as opposed to the Articles of Confederation, I would argue this as appropriate. His first term encompassed the 1st and 2nd United States Congresses both of which would be considered Pro-Administration or Federalist. As for the opinion of President Washington himself, as it relates to national indebtedness I offer the following quote once again from his farewell address:

"As a very important source of strength and security, cherish public credit. One method of preserving it is, to use it as sparingly as possible; avoiding occasions of expense by cultivating peace, but remembering also that timely disbursements to prepare for danger frequently prevent much greater disbursements to repel it; avoiding likewise the accumulation of debt, not only by shunning occasions of expense, but by vigorous exertions in time of peace to discharge the debts, which unavoidable wars may have occasioned, not ungenerously throwing upon posterity the burthen, which we ourselves ought to bear."

Our first fiscal year ended on 01 January 1791 and reflected all of 1790 and the last 8 months of 1789. Among the first actions of President Washington and the 1ˢᵗ United States Congress was the affirmation of debts that had been incurred under the auspices of the Confederation Congress which had been created by the Articles of Confederation. Therefore the Constitutional United States of America was born in debt and has been there, to varying degrees, ever since.

An important note: On 25 February 1791 the United States Congress chartered the First Bank of the United States. The charter was set for a 20-year expiration date. The Bank was created to handle the financial needs and requirements of the central government of the newly formed United States, which had previously been thirteen individual states with their own banks, currencies, financial institutions, and policies. The bank's charter expired in 1811 under President James Madison. The bill to recharter failed in the House of Representatives by one vote, 65 to 64, on 24 January 1811.

The building which housed The First Bank of the United States is now a National Historic Landmark located in Philadelphia, Pennsylvania within Independence National Historical Park.

The following table shows the national debt, along with the rate of change, through this first presidential term as well as Congresses 1 and 2:

Fiscal Year	Total Debt	Change	% Change
1791	$75,463,476.52		
1792	$77,227,924.66	$1,764,448.14	2.34%
1793	$80,358,634.04	$3,130,709.38	4.05%
Total		$4,895,157.52	6.49%

So here we have our first presidential administration and our first 2 Congresses adding 6.49% to the national debt. In my opinion neither of our two current major political parties have justifiable claim to the legacy of this, and several other administrations. In light of that fact our tally will include an "other" category for those administrations.

Administration	Increased Debt	Decreased Debt	Party Totals
Democrat			
Republican			
Other	1		1
Total	1		1

Totally off point, however being from Kentucky I thought it interesting, did you know that the first bourbon whiskey was distilled in 1789? Also in 1790 Swiss scientist Jacob Schweppe produced a carbonated beverage in London.

In 1793 President Washington was inaugurated for his personal second term and the second presidential term in total for our country. This inauguration occurred in Philadelphia making President Washington our only President to be inaugurated in two different cities. In his second term President Washington was confronted with a 3rd Congress that was split with those considered Pro-Administration in the Senate and others considered Anti-Administration in the House. By the seating of the 4th Congress in 1795 the Federalist were in control in the Senate and the Democratic-Republicans had control of the House. In effect the same ideological divide as the 3rd Congress, only now they had coalesced into official political parties under the tutorship of Alexander Hamilton, then Secretary of the Treasury, and Vice-President Thomas Jefferson respectively.

Just a few items of interest from this time period are; 1793 seeing the first hot air balloon flight in the US, the forerunner of our real estate commercial from chapter 2; 1794 has the US Army quelling the Whiskey Rebellion right here in the United States; 1795 finds Jose Maria Guadalupe Cuervo receiving the first license to produce tequila in New Spain; 1796 finds the first experimental use of the smallpox vaccine.

Now I'm certain that everyone is burning to know how this second administration performed with regard to the national debt, so without further adieu, please turn the page to take a look at our next table where this administration's results are offered for your consideration.

Fiscal Year	Total Debt	Change	% Change
1793	$80,358,634.04		
1794	$78,427,404.77	-$1,931,229.27	-2.40%
1795	$80,747,587.39	$2,320,182.62	2.96%
1796	$83,762,172.07	$3,014,584.68	3.73%
1797	$82,064,479.33	-$1,697,692.74	-2.03%
Total		$1,705,845.29	2.12%

As you can plainly see, 2 of the 4 years the debt was paid down, and the 2 remaining years it increased. The total for the 4 year term was an increase of $1,705,845.09 or 2.12%. Incidentally, over the course of both Washington administrations taken as a whole, we suffered a debt increase of $6,601,002.81 or 8.0%. Lets add this administration to our tally, shall we:

Administration	Increased Debt	Decreased Debt	Party Totals
Democrat			
Republican			
Other	2		2
Total	2		2

Now we will move on to our 3rd presidential term, our 2nd President, in the person of, President John Adams. This first and only administration for President Adams ran from 04 March 1797 through 04 March 1801 and encompassed the 5th and 6th United States Congresses. The President and the majorities in both Congresses were Federalists.

In his first address to Congress on 23 November 1797 President Adams made his feelings on the national debt clear as shown by the following quote:

"The consequences arising from the continual accumulation of public debts in other countries ought to admonish us to be careful to prevent their growth in our own. "

Fiscal Year	Total Debt	Change	% Change
1797	$82,064,479.33		
1798	$79,228,529.12	-$2,835,950.21	-3.46%
1799	$78,408,669.77	-$819,859.35	-1.03%
1800	$82,976,294.35	$4,567,624.58	5.83%
1801	$83,038,050.80	$61,756.45	0.07%
Total		$973,571.47	1.19%

Now for a short interlude into the totally irrelevant but hopefully entertaining. What was happening around the planet during this period of time?

Well, since you asked, 1797 finds the first US Senator being expelled in the person of William Blount from Tennessee, the charge was treason, centering on a plan to incite the Creek and Cherokee to aid the British in conquering the Spanish territory of West Florida ; 1798 sees the French give us one of the most recognizable political traditions of our time when the French Council of 500 introduces the idea of sitting left or right of center based upon political ideology; 1799 finds the British giving us something we will find all too familiar in 21st century America when their parliament passes the world's first income tax; 1800 sees the publication of "Life of Washington" by Mason Locke, the largely fictional biography of President George Washington, providing us with many myths concerning our first President, such as, cutting down the cherry tree and the ever popular "I can not tell a lie".

OK, back to the business. As you can see from the preceding table, President Adams allowed the national debt to increase. Not by very much but it did increase.

Let's update our tally and then move on.

Administration	Increased Debt	Decreased Debt	Party Totals
Democrat			
Republican			
Other	3		3
Total	3		3

We are now ready to take a look at our 4th presidential term, the 1st of 2 terms for President Thomas Jefferson, our 3rd President. This term spans from 04 March 1801 through 04 March 1805, and also encompasses the 7th and 8th United States Congresses. The majority party in both houses for both Congresses was the Democratic-Republican party, of which President Jefferson was not only a member, but the founder.

We have, at this point, read quotes from both President Washington and President Adams concerning their view of public indebtedness. The following paragraph is taken from a letter President Jefferson wrote to Samuel Kercheval in the year 1816. While it is a bit lengthy, personally, I believe it bares careful consideration. The full letter appears in appendix 3.

"I have thrown out these as loose heads of amendment, for consideration and correction; and their object is to secure self-government by the republicanism of our constitution, as well as by the spirit of the people; and to nourish and perpetuate that spirit. I am not among those who fear the people. They, and not the rich, are our dependence for continued freedom. And to preserve their independence, we must not let our rulers load us with perpetual debt. We must make our election between economy and liberty, or profusion and servitude. If we run into such debts, as that we must be taxed in our meat and in our drink, in our necessaries and our comforts, in our labors and our amusements, for our callings and our creeds, as the people of England are, our people, like them, must come to labor sixteen hours in the twenty-four, give the earnings of fifteen of these to the government for their debts and daily expenses; and the sixteenth being insufficient to afford us bread, we must live, as they now do, on oatmeal and potatoes; have no time to think, no means of calling the mismanagers to account; but be glad to obtain subsistence by hiring ourselves to rivet their chains on the necks of our fellow-sufferers. Our landholders, too, like theirs, retaining indeed the title and stewardship of estates called theirs, but held really in trust for the treasury, must wander, like theirs, in foreign countries, and be contented with penury, obscurity, exile, and the glory of the nation. This example reads to us the salutary lesson,

that private fortunes are destroyed by public as well as by private extravagance. And this is the tendency of all human governments. A departure from principle in one instance becomes a precedent for a second; that second for a third; and so on, till the bulk of the society is reduced to be mere automatons of misery, and to have no sensibilities left but for sinning and suffering. Then begins, indeed, the bellum omnium in omnia, which some philosophers observing to be so general in this world, have mistaken it for the natural, instead of the abusive state of man. And the fore horse of this frightful team is public debt. Taxation follows that, and in its train wretchedness and oppression. "

Wow, let that one sink in for a moment, in fact I would ask that you go back and read it a second, maybe even a third time. Pretty good Nostradamus impression, don't you think? Don't forget the full letter appears in appendix number 3 at the rear of this book.

Now it bears remembering that the party that was founded by President Jefferson, the Democratic-Republicans, are the majority party in both houses of Congress. You have just read a quote from President Jefferson himself in which he, in pretty strong terms, lays out his opinion of national indebtedness and it's affect upon a government, and more importantly, the citizens that government is intended to responsibly govern. We saw rather negative opinions of debt from both President Washington and President Adams, however, all 3 administrations presided over by those 2 Presidents allowed the national debt to increase. How will President Jefferson fair in his first term? How is that for an attempt to build suspense?

As for a few events which occurred around the planet in this time period we offer the following. 1802 finds the publication of the first American comic book, it's title was The Wasp. 1803 sees the first public library open in Connecticut. You think today's politics are rough and tumble? In 1804 then Vice President Aaron Burr, mortally wounded former Secretary of the Treasury Alexander Hamilton in a duel. Just so we all understand, these guys willingly, guns in hand, marched in opposite directions some number of paces and then turned and fired upon one another. By the way, this is not the last time we will find our sitting or future government officials engaging in this activity. What do you think these men of the 19th century might do in response to the political advertising and commentary here in the 21st century. Interesting question to ponder don't ya think. 1805 finds the premiere of Beethoven's "Eroica", which Beethoven himself conducted.

Okay, welcome back, hope you enjoyed our little interlude. Now back to the business at hand.

Fiscal Year	Total Debt	Change	% Change
1801	$83,038,050.80		
1802	$80,712,632.25	-$2,325,418.55	-2.80%
1803	$77,054,686.40	-$3,657,945.85	-4.53%
1804	$86,427,120.88	$9,372,434.48	12.16%
1805	$82,312,150.50	-$4,114,970.38	-4.76%
Total		-$725,900.30	-0.87%

Now we will add this administration to our running tally. Again, in my opinion, neither the modern Republicans nor Democrats can legitimately claim this administration as their own so we will remain in the others column.

Administration	Increased Debt	Decreased Debt	Party Totals
Democrat			
Republican			
Other	3	1	4
Total	3	1	4

There you have it! The 1st administration for President Jefferson, the 4th presidential term overall, and the 1st administration to actually reduce the national debt.

Moving on to the 2nd administration for our 3rd President, President Thomas Jefferson, and our 5th presidential term overall. This administration began on 04 March 1805 and ended on 04 March 1809. It encompassed the 9th and 10th United States Congresses. The majority party in both houses of

Congress for both the 9th and 10th Congresses was Democratic-Republican once again. Will this 2nd Jefferson term produce a second consecutive reduction of the national debt?

And now for a few words from our sponsor. 1806 finds future President Andrew Jackson killing Charles Dickinson in a duel. Because dueling was outlawed in Tennessee, the two men met in Kentucky on 30 May. Dickinson was widely considered a expert marksman so, legend has it, Jackson formulated a very risky strategy. He would allow Dickinson to fire first, hoping that he would rush a bit, thereby producing an errant shot. Then, assuming he were still alive, Jackson would be free to take careful aim at Dickinson. These guys played for keeps! You think folks might be a bit more civilized, if this practice was still acceptable today? I'm just saying.

1807 gives us the first street in London to be lit by gas lights. The name of the street is Pall Mall, and yes, the cigarette is named for it. 1808 finds the Rum Rebellion in Australia. A successful armed takeover of the government in Australia. Humph, our revolution began with the tea party, we had a whiskey rebellion, and Australia had a rum rebellion. Moral of this story, today's politicians may want to reconsider taxing soft drinks, history suggests people get very upset when access to their drink of choice is threatened. 04 January 1809 has the birth of Louis Braille in Coupvray, France.

Now never mind that we don't have a sponsor and the preceding interlude wasn't really a commercial, nor even a television show for that matter, but you didn't think we would go directly to the answer did you? Where's the fun in that? Haven't you seen American Idol?

Fiscal Year	Total Debt	Change	% Change
1805	$82,312,150.50		
1806	$75,723,270.66	-$6,588,879.84	-8.00%
1807	$69,218,398.64	-$6,504,872.02	-8.59%
1808	$65,196,317.97	-$4,022,080.67	-5.81%
1809	$57,023,192.09	-$8,173,125.88	-12.54%
Total		-$25,288,958.41	-30.72%

I hope it was worth the wait. Now for the tally through 5 presidential terms and 3 Presidents.

Administration	Increased Debt	Decreased Debt	Party Totals
Democrat			
Republican			
Other	3	2	5
Total	3	2	5

As you can see President Jefferson gave us 2 consecutive administrations that successfully reduced our national debt. The second by just over 30%. I think this is sufficient evidence to conclude that it is possible. It certainly seems congruent with the previous quote, as well as this one:

"I, however, place economy among the first and most important republican virtues, and public debt as the greatest of the dangers to be feared."

Now on to President number 4, presidential term 6, in the person of, President James Madison. President Madison was a member of Jefferson's Democratic-Republican party, and this is the 1st of 2 terms for him. It encompassed the 11th and 12th Congresses and it began on 04 March 1809 and ran through 04 March 1813. The majority party in both houses of Congress was the Democratic-Republican party. In keeping with previous administrations lets see what President Madison had to say concerning the national debt:

"I go on the principle that a public debt is a public curse, and in a Republican Government a greater curse than any other"

One interesting note, legend has it that President Madison was the first President to be inaugurated wearing clothing that had been made in America. I can't really say why, but I personally found that to be something of a surprise.

1810 sees the first Oktoberfest, as the Bavarian royalty invites the citizens of Munich to join the celebration of the marriage of Crown Prince Ludwig of Bavaria to Princess Therese von Sachsen-Hildburghausen. 1811 sees future President, Gen. William Henry Harrison, defeat the Native Americans of the Tecumesh Confederation in the Battle of Tippecanoe. In 1812 then governor of Massachusetts, Elbridge Gerry gives us the term "gerrymandering" when he signs a redistricting plan designed to favor the Democratic-Republican party in the coming elections. 1813 has the first publication of Pride and Prejudice, by Jane Austen, in the United Kingdom.

Meanwhile, back at the bat cave...

Fiscal Year	Total Debt	Change	% Change
1809	$57,023,192.09		
1810	$53,173,217.52	-$3,849,974.57	-6.75%
1811	$48,005,587.76	-$5,167,629.76	-9.72%
1812	$45,209,737.90	-$2,795,849.86	-5.82%
1813	$55,962,827.57	$10,753,089.67	23.78%
Total		-$1,060,364.52	-1.86%

Now for the tally through 6 presidential terms and 4 presidents.

Administration	Increased Debt	Decreased Debt	Party Totals
Democrat			
Republican			
Other	3	3	6
Total	3	3	6

As you can see, we have now evened the tally of administrations increasing vs. decreasing the national debt at 3 each.

On to the 7th presidential term overall, and the 2nd of 2 for President Madison, our fourth President. This administration ran from 04 March 1813 through 04 March 1817 encompassing the 13th and 14th United States Congresses. The majority in both houses of Congress, of both Congresses, was the Democratic-Republican party, sound familiar, those guys are really on a role here.

For the conspiracy theorist among you, 1814 sees the first Knights Templar grand encampment in US held in New York City. 1815 may seem a strange year to find the last battle of a war that ended in 1814, however the final battle wasn't fought until January of 1815 at the Battle of New Orleans , The battle was an American victory led by future President, Major General Andrew Jackson. 1816 sees the Second Bank of the United States chartered by Congress. The primary reason that the Second Bank of the United States was chartered was that in the War of 1812, the U.S. experienced severe inflation and had difficulty in financing military operations. Subsequently, the credit and borrowing status of the United States were at their lowest levels since its founding. Sound familiar? 1817 finds the opening of the first private mental health hospital in the United States, the Asylum for the Relief of Persons Deprived of the Use of Their Reason, in Philadelphia, Pennsylvania. Just try putting that name on the breast pocket of a golf shirt.

Back to business, how did President Madison fair in his 2nd administration?

Fiscal Year	Total Debt	Change	% Change
1813	$55,962,827.57		
1814	$81,487,846.24	$25,525,018.67	45.61%
1815	$99,833,660.15	$18,345,813.91	22.51%
1816	$127,334,933.74	$27,501,273.59	27.55%
1817	$123,491,965.16	-$3,842,968.58	-3.02%
Total		$67,529,137.59	120.67%

Now for the tally through 7 presidential terms and 4 Presidents.

Administration	Increased Debt	Decreased Debt	Party Totals
Democrat			
Republican			
Other	4	3	7
Total	4	3	7

Lets meet our 5th President and take a look at our 8th presidential term. President James Monroe, Democratic-Republican, serving in the 1st of his 2 terms. This term began on 04 March 1817 and ran through 04 March 1821. The majority party in both houses of Congress of the 15th and 16th Congresses was the Democratic-Republican party. While he did not extoll the virtues nor delineate the evils of the national debt, as did his predecessors, President Monroe did share the following opinion on the finances of the government in his first inaugural address.

"The Executive is charged officially in the Departments under it with the disbursement of the public money, and is responsible for the faithful application of it to the purposes for which it is raised. The Legislature is the watchful guardian over the public purse. It is its duty to see that the disbursement has been honestly made."

Back to the largely useless, but hopefully entertaining, for a moment or two. 1818 begins with the official reopening of the White House. 1819 sees the "swift walker", fore runner of the bicycle, introduced to the United States in New York City. So, you think taxes are bad now do ya, how about this one? In 1820 Missouri imposed a $1.00 bachelor tax on unmarried men between 21 & 50 years of age. In 1821 The Foundation of the Mercantile Library Association was instigated by the New York Chamber of Commerce, which placed newspaper advertisements asking merchant clerks to meet at a local coffee house to discuss forming an organization based on the Mercantile Library in Boston, which had been created earlier that year. The purpose of the new organization was to provide the city's growing population of clerks with an alternative to what were considered to be immoral entertainments and other vices of the city. We invent video games, they built libraries.

Back to business.

Fiscal Year	Total Debt	Change	% Change
1817	$123,491,965.16		
1818	$103,466,633.83	-$20,025,331.33	-16.22%
1819	$95,529,648.28	-$7,936,985.55	-7.67%
1820	$91,015,566.15	-$4,514,082.13	-4.73%
1821	$89,987,427.66	-$1,028,138.49	-1.13%
Total		-$33,504,537.50	-27.13%

Now for the tally through 8 presidential terms and 5 Presidents.

Administration	Increased Debt	Decreased Debt	Party Totals
Democrat			
Republican			
Other	4	4	8
Total	4	4	8

On to presidential term number 9, the 2nd of 2, for President Monroe. This term began on 04 March 1821 and runs through 04 March 1825, and encompasses the 17th and 18th Congresses. The majority party in both houses for both of these Congresses was Democratic-Republican. Don't suppose that was much of a surprise at this point.

1822 finds Charles Graham of NY receiving a patent for artificial teeth. 1823 has R J Tyers receive a patent for roller skates. 1824 has the washing machine patented by Noah Cushing of Quebec. 1825 sees Ezra Daggett &

nephew Thomas Kensett patent food storage in tin cans. A little bit of inventors corner here in the first quarter of the 19th century.

Back to our topic.

Fiscal Year	Total Debt	Change	% Change
1821	$89,987,427.66		
1822	$93,546,676.98	$3,559,249.32	3.96%
1823	$90,875,877.28	-$2,670,799.70	-2.86%
1824	$90,269,777.77	-$606,099.51	-0.67%
1825	$83,788,432.71	-$6,481,345.06	-7.18%
Total		-$6,198,994.95	-6.89%

Now for the tally through 9 presidential terms and 5 Presidents.

Administration	Increased Debt	Decreased Debt	Party Totals
Democrat			
Republican			
Other	4	5	9
Total	4	5	9

On to the 10th presidential term and our 6th President, in the person of President John Quincy Adams. John Quincy was the son of our 2nd President, John Adams. Together they form the first father/son combination to both serve as President of the United States. This term began on 04 March 1825 and ran through 04 March 1829, encompassing the 19th and 20th Congresses. The Democratic-Republican party has at this point fractured into several factions, one of which would form the basis for the modern Democratic party. At this point, however, they were commonly known as

Jacksonian or Anti-Jacksonian. The 19th Congress was split between these 2 factions as the Senate was considered Jacksonian and the House being Anti-Jacksonian. The 20th Congress found both houses in the Jacksonian camp.

Continuing with the inventors theme for a moment 1826 finds John Walker inventing the friction match in England. 1827 sees Joseph Dixon begin manufacturing lead pencils. 1828 provides one of my favorites when Casparus van Wooden patents chocolate milk powder.

We now return you to the program in progress.

Fiscal Year	Total Debt	Change	% Change
1825	$83,788,432.71		
1826	$81,054,059.99	-$2,734,372.72	-3.26%
1827	$73,987,357.20	-$7,066,702.79	-8.72%
1828	$67,475,043.87	-$6,512,313.33	-8.80%
1829	$58,421,413.67	-$9,053,630.20	-13.42%
Total		-$25,367,019.04	-30.28%

Now for the tally through 10 presidential terms and 6 Presidents.

Administration	Increased Debt	Decreased Debt	Party Totals
Democrat			
Republican			
Other	4	6	10
Total	4	6	10

There we have another administration to seriously pay down the national debt. As you can see from the table above we actually have more administrations reducing the debt than increasing it. Hard to imagine in today's environment isn't it.

Important Note: There is another significant event surrounding this election for President. If you recall, way back in the prologue, while attempting to explain part of my motivations for writing this book, I mentioned a sense that a lot of the charges and counter charges being leveled by both sides of our current political class didn't seem quite accurate. Here is an extreme case in point. This election is widely known as the first in which the winner of the popular vote, Andrew Jackson with 153,544 vs. Adams' with 108,740, did not win the presidency due to the electoral college. While this is in fact true it is not the **"whole truth"**.

Not only did Jackson win the popular vote he also received more electoral college votes than did Adams, Jackson 99 vs. Adams 84. This tally did not however provide a majority as required by the Constitution. Accordingly, the election was decided by the House of Representatives, as provided by the 12th Amendment to the Constitution, which selected Adams on the first ballot. Afterward, allegations of a "corrupt bargain" were leveled at Adams and then Speaker of the House, Kentucky's own, Henry Clay. This was prompted by Clay's appointment to the position of Secretary of State in the Adams administration, which the Jackson supporters saw as evidence of the fact.

Lastly, and while even less well know and I believe much more significant, was the fact that this is the first presidential election for which a national popular vote had even been held. That's right, we are up to President number 6 and election number 10, and we have had our first nation wide popular vote. Please remember this very important point, which is illustrated completely in this event. The system of government created by the Constitution is **not** a **democracy,** as in **direct democracy**! It does create a form of a democracy called a **representative republic,** which requires some further description. This means that rather than voting directly for or against someone, we, the voting public, vote for a **body of representation**, in this case the electoral college, who are then empowered to make decisions on our behalf.

Enough about that, lets move on, we still have a lot to cover. We are now ready to look at the 11th presidential term which was filled by President Andrew Jackson, our 7th President. We can also now welcome the birth of one of our two current major political parties, the Democrats. This administration began on 04 March 1829 and ran through 04 March 1833. It encompasses the 21st and 22nd Congresses which found both houses, in both Congresses, with majorities in support of President Jackson.

President Jackson, was imminently quotable on many subjects, including the national debt. For an example of his opinion of the debt, I offer the following two quotes:

"I am one of those who do not believe that a national debt is a national blessing, but rather a curse to a republic; inasmuch as it is calculated to raise around the administration a moneyed aristocracy dangerous to the liberties of the country."

"It is to be regretted that the rich and powerful too often bend the acts of government to their selfish purposes."

Fiscal Year	Total Debt	Change	% Change
1829	$58,421,413.67		
1830	$48,565,406.50	-$9,856,007.17	-16.87%
1831	$39,123,191.68	-$9,442,214.82	-19.44%
1832	$24,322,235.18	-$14,800,956.50	-37.83%
1833	$7,001,698.83	-$17,320,536.35	-71.21%
Total		-$51,419,714.84	-88.02%

Now for the tally through 11 presidential terms and 7 Presidents.

Administration	Increased Debt	Decreased Debt	Party Totals
Democrat		1	1
Republican			0
Other	4	6	10
Total	4	7	11

Wow , an 88% reduction in the national debt over the course of a single 4 year administration.

Our next administration is the 12th presidential term, and is the 2nd of 2 for President Jackson, our 7th President. This term runs from 04 March 1833 through 04 March 1837, and encompassed the 23rd and 24th Congresses. The majority party in the Senate for the 23rd Congress was considered Anti-Jacksonian, while the House was considered Jacksonian. Both houses in the 24th were considered Jacksonian majorities.

Fiscal Year	Total Debt	Change	% Change
1833	$7,001,698.83		
1834	$4,760,082.08	-$2,241,616.75	-32.02%
1835	$33,733.05	-$4,726,349.03	-99.29%
1836	$37,513.05	$3,780.00	11.21%
1837	$336,957.83	$299,444.78	798.24%
Total		-$6,664,741.00	-95.19%

Now for the tally through 12 presidential terms and 7 Presidents.

Administration	Increased Debt	Decreased Debt	Party Totals
Democrat		2	2
Republican			0
Other	4	6	10
Total	4	8	12

President Jackson with an 88% reduction in his 1st term followed by a 95% reduction in his 2nd term. In current times, we talk about reducing deficits over 10 years, President Jackson effectively retired the national debt in 8 years, reducing it by 99% over the course of his 8 years in office.

Our constitutional government is now 48 years old and, with thanks to Dave Ramsey for the phrase, "WE ARE DEBT FREE"! Hard to imagine with today's debt ceiling debates isn't it?

Moving on to President Martin Van Buren, our 8th President. This is our 13th presidential administration and ran from 04 March 1837 through 04 March 1841. President Van Buren, a Democrat, worked with Congresses 25 and 26 which had Democratic majorities in both houses of both Congresses.

President Van Buren offered this opinion on the role of the national debt:

"To avoid the necessity of a permanent debt and its inevitable consequences, I have advocated and endeavored to carry into effect the policy of confining the appropriations for the public service to such objects only as are clearly with the constitutional authority of the Federal Government."

So lets take a look at our results and see how we actually did during this administration.

Fiscal Year	Total Debt	Change	% Change
1837	$336,957.83		
1838	$3,308,124.07	$2,971,166.24	881.76%
1839	$10,434,221.14	$7,126,097.07	215.41%
1840	$3,573,343.82	-$6,860,877.32	-65.75%
1841	$5,250,875.54	$1,677,531.72	46.95%
Total		$4,913,917.71	1458.32%

Now for the tally through 13 presidential terms and 8 Presidents.

Administration	Increased Debt	Decreased Debt	Party Totals
Democrat	1	2	3
Republican			0
Other	4	6	10
Total	5	8	13

Well our freedom from debt didn't last very long. A very short 4 years later, our national debt was increased by a whopping 1,458.32%. Even though this percentage increase is huge, we are still well below the amount we owed after the first fiscal year for our constitutional government. Remember this one started with debt near 0. The trend over our first ½ century, while bumpy, is one of significant reduction of our national debt.

Moving on to our 14th presidential term, and for the first time, we loose a sitting President. President William Henry Harrison, a member of the Whig party, was elected as our 9th President. He was inaugurated on 04 March 1841 and died of pneumonia on 04 April 1841 at 68 years of age. Vice-President John Tyler ascended to the office of President, becoming President number 10, serving the remainder of this term which ended on 04 March 1845.

This administration worked with the 27th and 28th Congresses. The 27th Congress had the Whigs enjoying majority party status in both houses, while the 28th had a Whig majority in the Senate with a Democrat majority in the House. Additionally, the fiscal year was changed to July 1 in 1843.

1842 sees the 1st US child labor law regulating working hours passed in Massachusetts. 1843 teaches us that the more things change the more they stay the same when on 21 March Preacher William Miller of Mass. predicts "the world will end today". 1844 sees Samuel FB Morse tap out "What hath God wrought" sending the 1st message by telegraph. It's 29 January 1845, I'm scared and I'm not even there, nor is it Halloween, however Edgar Allen Poe publishes "The Raven" for the first time, on this date in New York City. One slightly more significant event from 1845 is that the Senate over rides a presidential veto.

Time to get back to our study.

Fiscal Year	Total Debt	Change	% Change
1841	$5,250,875.54		
1842	$13,594,480.73	$8,343,605.19	158.90%
1843	$20,201,226.27	$6,606,745.54	48.60%
1843	$32,742,922.00	$12,541,695.73	62.08%
1844	$23,461,652.50	-$9,281,269.50	-28.35%
1845	$15,925,303.01	-$9,281,269.50	-39.56%
Total		$10,674,427.47	203.29%

Now for the tally through 14 presidential terms and 10 Presidents.

Administration	Increased Debt	Decreased Debt	Party Totals
Democrat	1	2	3
Republican			0
Other	5	6	11
Total	6	8	14

Democrat James K. Polk is our 11th President and serves in the 15th presidential term, which ran from 04 March 1845 through 04 March 1849. This administration encompassed the 29th and 30th Congresses. The 29th Congress had the Democratic party holding majorities in both houses, while the 30th had a Democratic majority in the Senate, with a Whig majority in the House.

President Polk made his feelings about the national debt known in his inaugural address:

"Ours was intended to be a plain and frugal government, and I shall regard it to be my duty to recommend to Congress and, as far as the Executive is concerned, to enforce by all the means within my power the strictest economy in the expenditure of the public money which may be compatible with the public interests.

A national debt has become almost an institution of European monarchies. It is viewed in some of them as an essential prop to existing governments. Melancholy is the condition of that people whose government can be sustained only by a system which periodically transfers large amounts from the labor of the many to the coffers of the few. Such a system is incompatible with the ends for which our republican Government was instituted. Under a wise policy the debts contracted in our Revolution and during the War of 1812 have been happily extinguished. By a judicious application of the revenues not required for other necessary purposes, it is not doubted that the debt which has grown out of the circumstances of the last few years may be speedily paid off."

Fiscal Year	Total Debt	Change	% Change
1845	$15,925,303.01		
1846	$15,550,202.97	-$375,100.04	-2.36%
1847	$38,826,534.77	$23,276,331.80	149.69%
1848	$47,044,862.23	$8,218,327.46	21.17%
1849	$63,061,858.69	$16,016,996.46	34.05%
Total		$47,136,555.68	295.99%

Now for the tally through 15 presidential terms and11 Presidents.

Administration	Increased Debt	Decreased Debt	Party Totals
Democrat	2	2	4
Republican			0
Other	5	6	11
Total	7	8	15

We are now up to our 12th President, Zachary Taylor a member of the Whig party, and our 16th presidential term. For the second time we loose a sitting President, President Taylor is inaugurated on 04 March 1849 and dies of natural causes on 09 July 1850. He is succeeded by his Vice-President, our 13th President, Millard Fillmore who completes this term, ending on 04 March 1853. This administration worked with Congresses 31 and 32, both of which had Democratic majorities in both houses.

As for President Taylor's view of the national debt, I offer the following from his inaugural address:

"It shall be my study to recommend such constitutional measures to Congress as may be necessary and proper to secure encouragement and protection to the great interests of agriculture, commerce, and manufactures, to improve our rivers and harbors, to provide for the speedy extinguishment of the public debt, to enforce a strict accountability on the part of all officers of the Government and the utmost economy in all public expenditures."

As for President Fillmore, the following quote actually comes after his presidency and after the civil war in fact.

"Three years of civil war have desolated the fairest portion of our land; loaded the country with an enormous debt that the sweat of millions yet unborn must be taxed to pay; arrayed brother against brother, father against son in mortal combat; deluged our country with fraternal blood; whitened our battlefields with the bones of the slain; and darkened the sky with the pall of mourning."

Fiscal Year	Total Debt	Change	% Change
1849	$63,061,858.69		
1850	$63,452,773.55	$390,914.86	0.62%
1851	$68,304,796.02	$4,852,022.47	7.65%
1852	$66,199,341.71	-$2,105,454.31	-3.08%
1853	$59,803,117.70	-$6,396,224.01	-9.66%
Total		-$3,258,740.99	-5.17%

Now for the tally through 16 presidential terms and 13 Presidents.

Administration	Increased Debt	Decreased Debt	Party Totals
Democrat	2	2	4
Republican			0
Other	6	6	12
Total	8	8	16

President Franklin Pierce, our 14th President and a member of the Democratic party, served in the 17th presidential term. This term began on 04 March 1853 and ran through 04 March 1857. This administration encompassed the 33rd Congress with Democratic majorities in both houses, and the 34th Congress with a Democratic majority in the Senate, and a new party, the Opposition Coalition in the House.

President Pierce didn't speak on the virtues nor the evils of the national debt explicitly, so lets see how this administration fared.

Fiscal Year	Total Debt	Change	% Change
1853	$59,803,117.70		
1854	$42,242,222.42	-$17,560,895.28	-29.36%
1855	$35,586,956.56	-$6,655,265.86	-15.76%
1856	$31,972,537.90	-$3,614,418.66	-10.16%
1857	$28,699,831.85	-$3,272,706.05	-10.24%
Total		-$31,103,285.85	-52.01%

Now for the tally through 17 presidential terms and 14 Presidents.

Administration	Increased Debt	Decreased Debt	Party Totals
Democrat	2	3	5
Republican			0
Other	6	6	12
Total	8	9	17

That brings us to President James Buchanan, a Democrat, serving in the 18th presidential term, which ran from 04 March 1857 through 04 March 1861. This administration worked with the 35th and 36th Congresses. Both of these enjoyed Democratic majorities in the Senate, with no one party having a majority in the House. Once again President Buchanan didn't feature the national debt among topics for his speeches or his writings. Lets take a look and see just how this administration fared in regard to our topic of inquiry.

Fiscal Year	Total Debt	Change	% Change
1857	$28,699,831.85		
1858	$44,911,881.03	$16,212,049.18	56.49%
1859	$58,496,837.88	$13,584,956.85	30.25%
1860	$64,842,287.88	$6,345,450.00	10.85%
1861	$90,580,873.72	$25,738,585.84	39.69%
Total		$61,881,041.87	215.61%

Now for the tally through 18 presidential terms and 15 Presidents.

Administration	Increased Debt	Decreased Debt	Party Totals
Democrat	3	3	6
Republican			0
Other	6	6	12
Total	9	9	18

Now we move on to the 16th President serving in the 19h presidential term, the first Republican, President Abraham Lincoln. This term ran from 04 March 1861 through 04 March 1865. This administration had the 37th and 38th Congresses to work with, both of which enjoyed Republican majorities in both houses of Congress.

While President Lincoln didn't speak directly on the national debt he did offer this more general opinion of an economic system:

"The government should create, issue, and circulate all the currency and credits needed to satisfy the spending power of the government and the buying power of consumers. By adoption of these principles, the taxpayers will be saved immense sums of interest. Money will cease to be master and become the servant of humanity."

Fiscal Year	Total Debt	Change	% Change
1861	$90,580,873.72		
1862	$524,176,412.13	$433,595,538.41	478.68%
1863	$1,119,772,138.63	$595,595,726.50	113.63%
1864	$1,815,784,370.57	$696,012,231.94	62.16%
1865	$2,680,647,869.74	$864,863,499.17	47.63%
Total		$2,590,066,996.02	2859.40%

Now for the tally through 19 presidential terms and 16 Presidents.

Administration	Increased Debt	Decreased Debt	Party Totals
Democrat	3	3	6
Republican	1		1
Other	6	6	12
Total	10	9	19

Moving on to the 20th presidential term, the 2nd of 2 for our 16th President, Abraham Lincoln. This term begins on 04 March 1865 and ends abruptly with the assassination of President Lincoln on 14 April 1865. Vice-President Andrew Johnson, interestingly a Democrat, ascends to the office and becomes our 17th President, serving until 04 March 1869. This administration works with the 39th and 40th Congresses, both of which enjoyed Republican majorities in both houses. I consider this a Democrat administration. President Johnson offered the following.

"I hold it the duty of the executive to insist upon frugality in the expenditure, and a sparing economy is itself a great national source. "

Fiscal Year	Total Debt	Change	% Change
1865	$2,680,647,869.74		
1866	$2,773,236,173.69	$92,588,303.95	3.45%
1867	$2,678,126,103.87	-$95,110,069.82	-3.43%
1868	$2,611,687,851.19	-$66,438,252.68	-2.48%
1869	$2,588,452,213.94	-$23,235,637.25	-0.89%
Total		-$92,195,655.80	-3.44%

Now for the tally through 20 presidential terms and 17 Presidents.

Administration	Increased Debt	Decreased Debt	Party Totals
Democrat	3	4	7
Republican	1		1
Other	6	6	12
Total	10	10	20

On to the 21st term and our 18th President, the 1st of 2 terms for President Ulysses S. Grant, a Republican. This administration ran from 04 March 1869 through 04 March 1873 and encompassed the 41st and 42nd Congresses. Both houses of both Congresses enjoyed Republican majorities.

From President Grant I offer this excerpt from his 1st inaugural address.

"A great debt has been contracted in securing to us and our posterity the Union. The payment of this, principal and interest, as well as the return to a specie basis as soon as it can be accomplished without material detriment to the debtor class or to the country at large, must be provided for. To protect the national honor, every dollar of Government indebtedness should be paid in gold, unless otherwise expressly stipulated in the contract. Let it be understood that no repudiator of one farthing of our public debt will be trusted in public place, and it will go far toward strengthening a credit which ought to be the best in the world, and will ultimately enable us to replace the debt with bonds bearing less interest than we now pay. To this should be added a faithful collection of the revenue, a strict accountability to the Treasury for every dollar collected, and the greatest practicable retrenchment in expenditure in every department of Government. "

And from a bit further into this first inaugural address.

"How the public debt is to be paid or specie payments resumed is not so important as that a plan should be adopted and acquiesced in. A united determination to do is worth more than divided counsels upon the method of doing. "

In view of this largely unexpected lecture on the importance of retiring the national debt, unexpected because it was assumed he would direct most of his attention to reconciliation, lets take a look at the results from this administration.

Fiscal Year	Total Debt	Change	% Change
1869	$2,588,452,213.94		
1870	$2,480,672,427.81	-$107,779,786.13	-4.16%
1871	$2,353,211,332.32	-$127,461,095.49	-5.14%
1872	$2,253,251,328.78	-$99,960,003.54	-4.25%
1873	$2,234,482,993.20	-$18,768,335.58	-0.83%
Total		-$353,969,220.74	-13.67%

Now for the tally through 21 presidential terms and 18 Presidents.

Administration	Increased Debt	Decreased Debt	Party Totals
Democrat	3	4	7
Republican	1	1	2
Other	6	6	12
Total	10	11	21

On to the 22nd presidential term, the 2nd of 2 for our 18th President Ulysses S. Grant. This administration ran from 04 March 1873 through 04 March 1877 encompassing the 43rd and 44th Congresses. Both houses of the 43rd Congress had Republican majorities, while the 44th saw a Republican majority in the Senate, with a Democratic majority in the House.

The first term for President Grant had produced a significant reduction in the national debt. How do you think the second administration performed on this question? Lets turn the page and find out.

Fiscal Year	Total Debt	Change	% Change
1873	$2,234,482,993.20		
1874	$2,251,690,468.43	$17,207,475.23	0.77%
1875	$2,232,284,531.95	-$19,405,936.48	-0.86%
1876	$2,180,395,067.15	-$51,889,464.80	-2.32%
1877	$2,205,301,392.10	$24,906,324.95	1.14%
Total		-$29,181,601.10	-1.31%

Now for the tally through 22 presidential terms and 18 Presidents.

Administration	Increased Debt	Decreased Debt	Party Totals
Democrat	3	4	7
Republican	1	2	3
Other	6	6	12
Total	10	12	22

Whew! We have almost made it to end of chapter 3 and our first 19 Presidents. Hang in there, I know a trip through the table jungle isn't a lot of fun for most, but I think you will agree it was worthwhile when we arrive at the end of our journey, see ya then...

Now on to our 19th President serving in our 23rd administration, Republican Rutherford B. Hayes. This administration began 04 March 1877 and ran through 04 March 1881. It encompassed the 45th and 46th Congresses. The 45th Congress had a Republican majority in the Senate, with a Democratic majority in the House, while the 46th Congress enjoyed Democratic majorities in both houses.

Fiscal Year	Total Debt	Change	% Change
1877	$2,205,301,392.10		
1878	$2,256,205,892.53	$50,904,500.43	2.31%
1879	$2,349,567,482.04	$93,361,589.51	4.14%
1880	$2,120,415,370.63	-$229,152,111.41	-9.75%
1881	$2,069,013,569.58	-$51,401,801.05	-2.42%
Total		-$136,287,822.52	-6.18%

Now for the tally through 23 presidential terms and 19 Presidents.

Administration	Increased Debt	Decreased Debt	Party Totals
Democrat	3	4	7
Republican	1	3	4
Other	6	6	12
Total	10	13	23

Congratulations, you have made it through the first of two, admittedly, data heavy chapters. I hope you have learned a few things you might not have known, and had a least a little enjoyment in the process.

While our national debt has been increased from the founding of our constitutional government to this point, I think you will agree there seems to be a universal understanding and execution of President Washington's advice from his farewell address:

"....but by vigorous exertions in time of peace to discharge the debts, which unavoidable wars may have occasioned, ..."

4 - 1789 – 1869
(PRESIDENTS 20 THROUGH 38 &
CONGRESSES 41 THROUGH 94)

"Nostalgia is a file that removes the rough edges from the good old days."

Doug Larson

Welcome to chapter number 4. We are now continuing our march through the pages of American history, at least as it relates to the performance of each administration verses the national debt. There is no real reason for beginning a new chapter at this point other than an effort to break this into more digestible blocks of information. Hopefully you have had time to fix a sandwich and get yourself a fresh cup of coffee, or Mtn. Dew as it were, cause here we go again.

President James A. Garfield, our 20th President, serving in our 24th presidential term. President Garfield is our 2nd President to succumb to assassination as he is shot on 02 July and passes away on 19 September of 1881. At this time President Chester A Arthur becomes our 21st President serving out the remainder of this term, which began on 04 March 1881 and runs through 04 March 1885, encompassing the 47th and 48th United States Congresses. While both Garfield and Arthur were Republicans, the 47th Congress enjoyed a Democratic majority in the Senate with a Republican majority in the House, while the 48th had a Republican majority in the Senate with a Democratic majority in the House.

For President Garfield I offer the following quotation:

"He who controls the money supply of a nation controls the nation."

Chester A. Arthur offered the following:

"The extravagant expenditure of public money is an evil not to be measured by the value of that money to the people who are taxed for it. "

Fiscal Year	Total Debt	Change	% Change
1881	$2,069,013,569.58		
1882	$1,918,312,994.03	-$150,700,575.55	-7.28%
1883	$1,884,171,728.07	-$34,141,265.96	-1.78%
1884	$1,830,528,923.57	-$53,642,804.50	-2.85%
1885	$1,863,964,873.14	$33,435,949.57	1.83%
Total		-$205,048,696.44	-9.91%

Now for the tally through 24 presidential terms and 21 Presidents.

Administration	Increased Debt	Decreased Debt	Party Totals
Democrat	3	4	7
Republican	1	4	5
Other	6	6	12
Total	10	14	24

President Grover Cleveland, Democrat and our 22nd President, serving in the 25th presidential term. Beginning on 04 March 1885 and running through 04 March 1889. Encompassing the 49th and 50th Congresses. Both Congresses had Republican majorities in the Senate with Democrat majorities in the House.

One of my favorite quotes from President Cleveland appears below:

"He mocks the people who proposes that the government shall protect the rich and that they in turn will care for the laboring poor."

Fiscal Year	Total Debt	Change	% Change
1885	$1,863,964,873.14		
1886	$1,775,063,013.78	-$88,901,859.36	-4.77%
1887	$1,657,602,592.63	-$117,460,421.15	-6.62%
1888	$1,692,858,984.58	$35,256,391.95	2.13%
1889	$1,619,052,922.23	-$73,806,062.35	-4.36%
Total		-$244,911,950.91	-13.14%

Now for the tally through 25 presidential terms and 22 Presidents.

Administration	Increased Debt	Decreased Debt	Party Totals
Democrat	3	5	8
Republican	1	4	5
Other	6	6	12
Total	10	15	25

President Benjamin Harrison, a Republican and our 23rd President, serving in our 26 presidential administration. This term begins on 04 March 1889 and runs through 04 March 1893 covering the 51st and 52nd Congresses. The 51st had a Republican majority in both houses while the 52nd had Republicans in the Senate with Democrats in the House.

A favorite quote from President Harrison.

"I pity the man who wants a coat so cheap that the man or woman who produces the cloth will starve in the process. "

Fiscal Year	Total Debt	Change	% Change
1889	$1,619,052,922.23		
1890	$1,552,140,204.73	-$66,912,717.50	-4.13%
1891	$1,545,996,591.61	-$6,143,613.12	-0.40%
1892	$1,588,464,144.63	$42,467,553.02	2.75%
1893	$1,545,985,686.13	-$42,478,458.50	-2.67%
Total		-$73,067,236.10	-4.51%

Now for the tally through 26 presidential terms and 23 Presidents.

Administration	Increased Debt	Decreased Debt	Party Totals
Democrat	3	5	8
Republican	1	5	6
Other	6	6	12
Total	10	16	26

President Grover Cleveland, a Democrat and our 24th President, serving in the 27 presidential term. Yes, Grover Cleveland is our 22nd and our 24th President, thus becoming the only President in our history to serve 2 terms non-sequentially. This term begins on 04 March 1893 and runs through 04 March 1897, and encompassed the 53rd and 54th Congresses. The 53rd Congress had Democratic majorities in both houses while the 54th had Republican majorities in both houses.

President Cleveland was imminently quotable, here is another of my favorites:

"I would rather the man who presents something for my consideration subject me to a zephyr of truth and a gentle breeze of responsibility rather than blow me down with a curtain of hot wind. "

Fiscal Year	Total Debt	Change	% Change
1893	$1,545,985,686.13		
1894	$1,632,253,636.68	$86,267,950.55	5.58%
1895	$1,676,120,983.25	$43,867,346.57	2.69%
1896	$1,769,840,323.40	$93,719,340.15	5.59%
1897	$1,817,672,665.90	$47,832,342.50	2.70%
Total		$271,686,979.77	17.57%

Now for the tally through 27 presidential terms and 24 Presidents.

Administration	Increased Debt	Decreased Debt	Party Totals
Democrat	4	5	9
Republican	1	5	6
Other	6	6	12
Total	11	16	27

President William McKinley, a Republican and our 25th President, serving in our 28th presidential term. Beginning on 04 March 1897 and running through 04 March 1901, encompassing the 55th and 56th Congresses. Both Congresses had Republican majorities in both houses.

One of my favorite quotes from President McKinley:

"Let us ever remember that our interest is in concord, not in conflict; and that our real eminence rests in the victories of peace, not those of war. "

Fiscal Year	Total Debt	Change	% Change
1897	$1,817,672,665.90		
1898	$1,796,531,995.90	-$21,140,670.00	-1.16%
1899	$1,991,927,306.92	$195,395,311.02	10.88%
1900	$2,136,961,091.67	$145,033,784.75	7.28%
1901	$2,143,326,933.89	$6,365,842.22	0.30%
Total		$325,654,267.99	17.92%

Now for the tally through 28 presidential terms and 25 Presidents.

Administration	Increased Debt	Decreased Debt	Party Totals
Democrat	4	5	9
Republican	2	5	7
Other	6	6	12
Total	12	16	28

President William McKinley, a Republican and our 25th President, serving in our 29^h presidential term. President McKinley succumb to an assassins bullets on 14 September 1901, becoming our 3rd President to be assassinated. President Theodore Roosevelt rose to the office becoming our 26th President and serving the remainder of this term which began on 04 March 1901 and ran through 04 March 1905, encompassing the 57th and 58th Congresses. Both Congresses had Republican majorities in both houses.

Another quote from President McKinley:

"War should never be entered upon until every agency of peace has failed. "

Fiscal Year	Total Debt	Change	% Change
1901	$2,143,326,933.89		
1902	$2,158,610,445.89	$15,283,512.00	0.71%
1903	$2,202,464,781.89	$43,854,336.00	2.03%
1904	$2,264,003,585.14	$61,538,803.25	2.79%
1905	$2,274,615,063.84	$10,611,478.70	0.47%
Total		$131,288,129.95	6.13%

Now for the tally through 29 presidential terms and 26 Presidents.

Administration	Increased Debt	Decreased Debt	Party Totals
Democrat	4	5	9
Republican	3	5	8
Other	6	6	12
Total	13	16	29

President Theodore Roosevelt, a Republican and our 26th President serving in our 30th presidential term. This administration begins on 04 March 1905 and runs through 04 March 1909, covering the 59th and 60th Congresses. Both Congresses had Republican majorities in both houses.

Here is one of my favorites from President Roosevelt:

"Appraisals are where you get together with your team leader and agree what an outstanding member of the team you are, how much your contribution has been valued, what massive potential you have and, in recognition of all this, would you mind having your salary halved. "

Fiscal Year	Total Debt	Change	% Change
1905	$2,274,615,063.84		
1906	$2,337,161,839.04	$62,546,775.20	2.75%
1907	$2,457,188,061.54	$120,026,222.50	5.14%
1908	$2,626,806,271.54	$169,618,210.00	6.90%
1909	$2,639,546,241.04	$12,739,969.50	0.48%
Total		$364,931,177.20	16.04%

Now for the tally through 30 presidential terms and 26 Presidents.

Administration	Increased Debt	Decreased Debt	Party Totals
Democrat	4	5	9
Republican	4	5	9
Other	6	6	12
Total	14	16	30

President William H. Taft, a Republican and our 27th President, serving in the 31st presidential term. This administration began on 04 March 1909 and ran through 04 March 1913, encompassing the 61st and 62nd Congresses. The 61st had Republican majorities in both houses while the 62nd had Republicans in the Senate and Democrats in the House.

A favorite quote from President Taft, and it's right on topic.

"I am afraid I am a constant disappointment to my party. The fact of the matter is, the longer I am president the less of a party man I seem to become."

Fiscal Year	Total Debt	Change	% Change
1909	$2,639,546,241.04		
1910	$2,652,665,838.04	$13,119,597.00	0.50%
1911	$2,765,600,606.69	$112,934,768.65	4.26%
1912	$2,868,373,874.16	$102,773,267.47	3.72%
1913	$2,916,204,913.66	$47,831,039.50	1.67%
Total		$276,658,672.62	10.48%

Now for the tally through 31 presidential terms and 27 Presidents.

Administration	Increased Debt	Decreased Debt	Party Totals
Democrat	4	5	9
Republican	5	5	10
Other	6	6	12
Total	15	16	31

President Woodrow Wilson, a Democrat and our 28th President, serving in the 32nd presidential term. This term began on 04 March 1913 and ran through 04 March 1917, encompassing the 63rd and 64th Congresses. Both of these Congresses have Democratic majorities in both houses.

President Wilson is another in a long list of very quotable Presidents, he also seemed to have a great sense of humor. We will start with one that is a little more serious:

"Liberty has never come from Government. Liberty has always come from the subjects of it. The history of liberty is a history of limitations of governmental power, not the increase of it. "

Fiscal Year	Total Debt	Change	% Change
1913	$2,916,204,913.66		
1914	$2,912,499,269.16	-$3,705,644.50	-0.13%
1915	$3,058,136,873.16	$145,637,604.00	5.00%
1916	$3,609,244,262.16	$551,107,389.00	18.02%
1917	$5,717,770,279.52	$2,108,526,017.36	58.42%
Total		$2,801,565,365.86	96.07%

Now for the tally through 32 presidential terms and 28 Presidents.

Administration	Increased Debt	Decreased Debt	Party Totals
Democrat	5	5	10
Republican	5	5	10
Other	6	6	12
Total	16	16	32

President Woodrow Wilson, a Democrat and our 28th President, serving in the 32nd presidential term. This term began on 04 March 1917 and ran through 04 March 1921, encompassing the 65th and 66th Congresses. The 65th had Democratic majorities in both houses, while the 66th had Republican majorities in both houses.

Now for one of the more humorous quotes I mentioned earlier:

"I have long enjoyed the friendship and companionship of Republicans because I am by instinct a teacher, and I would like to teach them something."

Fiscal Year	Total Debt	Change	% Change
1917	$5,717,770,279.52		
1918	$14,592,161,414.00	$8,874,391,134.48	155.21%
1919	$27,390,970,113.12	$12,798,808,699.12	87.71%
1920	$25,952,456,406.16	-$1,438,513,706.96	-5.25%
1921	$23,977,450,552.54	-$1,975,005,853.62	-7.61%
Total		$18,259,680,273.02	319.35%

Now for the tally through 33 presidential terms and 28 Presidents.

Administration	Increased Debt	Decreased Debt	Party Totals
Democrat	6	5	11
Republican	5	5	10
Other	6	6	12
Total	17	16	33

President Warren G. Harding, a Republican and our 29th President, serving in the 34th presidential term. This administration begins on 04 March 1921, however President Harding dies of natural causes on 02 August 1923. President Calvin Coolidge ascends to the office, as our 30th President, and serves to the completion of this term on 04 March 1925. This administration works with the 67th and 68th Congresses. Both Congresses had a Republican majority in both houses.

President Harding was at least an honest man:

"I don't know what to do or where to turn in this taxation matter. Somewhere there must be a book that tells all about it, where I could go to straighten it out in my mind. But I don't know where the book is, and maybe I couldn't read it if I found it."

Fiscal Year	Total Debt	Change	% Change
1921	$23,977,450,552.54		
1922	$22,963,381,708.31	-$1,014,068,844.23	-4.23%
1923	$22,349,707,365.36	-$613,674,342.95	-2.67%
1924	$21,250,812,989.49	-$1,098,894,375.87	-4.92%
1925	$20,516,193,887.90	-$734,619,101.59	-3.46%
Total		-$3,461,256,664.64	-14.44%

Now for the tally through 34 presidential terms and 30 Presidents.

Administration	Increased Debt	Decreased Debt	Party Totals
Democrat	6	5	11
Republican	5	6	11
Other	6	6	12
Total	17	17	34

President Calvin Coolidge, a Republican and our 30th President, took office upon the death of President Harding and was then elected for the 35th presidential term. This administration began on 04 March 1925 and ran through 04 March 1929, encompassing the 69th and 70th Congresses. Both Congresses had Republican majorities in both houses.

President Coolidge left a lot of quotable moments even though he spoke of restraining ones speech:

"Little progress can be made by merely attempting to repress what is evil. Our great hope lies in developing what is good."

Fiscal Year	Total Debt	Change	% Change
1925	$20,516,193,887.90		
1926	$19,643,216,315.19	-$872,977,572.71	-4.26%
1927	$18,511,906,931.85	-$1,131,309,383.34	-5.76%
1928	$17,604,293,201.43	-$907,613,730.42	-4.90%
1929	$16,931,088,484.10	-$673,204,717.33	-3.82%
Total		-$3,585,105,403.80	-17.47%

Now for the tally through 35 presidential terms and 30 Presidents.

Administration	Increased Debt	Decreased Debt	Party Totals
Democrat	6	5	11
Republican	5	7	12
Other	6	6	12
Total	17	18	35

President Herbert Hoover, a Republican and our 31st President, serving in the 36 presidential term. This administration began on 04 March 1929 running through 04 March 1933, encompassing the 71st and 72nd Congresses. The 71st had Republican majorities in both houses, while the 72nd had a Republican Senate and a Democratic House.

I just had to include this quote from President Hoover, I expect the reason will be self-evident:

"Blessed are the young for they shall inherit the national debt."

Fiscal Year	Total Debt	Change	% Change
1929	$16,931,088,484.10		
1930	$16,185,309,831.43	-$745,778,652.67	-4.40%
1931	$16,801,281,491.71	$615,971,660.28	3.81%
1932	$19,487,002,444.13	$2,685,720,952.42	15.99%
1933	$22,538,672,560.15	$3,051,670,116.02	15.66%
Total		$5,607,584,076.05	33.12%

Now for the tally through 36 presidential terms and 31 Presidents.

Administration	Increased Debt	Decreased Debt	Party Totals
Democrat	6	5	11
Republican	6	7	13
Other	6	6	12
Total	18	18	36

President Franklin D. Roosevelt, a Democrat and our 32nd President, serving in the 37th presidential term. This administration began on 04 March 1933 running through 04 March 1937, encompassing the 73rd and 74th Congresses. Both houses of both Congresses had Democratic majorities.

The most difficult part of this exercise was picking the quotes from President Roosevelt to include:

"Competition has been shown to be useful up to a certain point and no further, but cooperation, which is the thing we must strive for today, begins where competition leaves off. "

Fiscal Year	Total Debt	Change	% Change
1933	$22,538,672,560.15		
1934	$27,053,141,414.48	$4,514,468,854.33	20.03%
1935	$28,700,892,624.53	$1,647,751,210.05	6.09%
1936	$33,778,543,493.73	$5,077,650,869.20	17.69%
1937	$36,424,613,732.29	$2,646,070,238.56	7.83%
Total		$13,885,941,172.14	61.61%

Now for the tally through 37 presidential terms and 32 Presidents.

Administration	Increased Debt	Decreased Debt	Party Totals
Democrat	7	5	12
Republican	6	7	13
Other	6	6	12
Total	19	18	37

President Franklin D. Roosevelt, a Democrat and our 32nd President, serving in the 38th presidential term. This administration began on 04 March 1937 running through 04 March 1941, encompassing the 75th and 76th Congresses. Both Congresses had Democratic majorities in both houses.

Another of my favorites from President Roosevelt:

"Don't forget what I discovered that over ninety percent of all national deficits from 1921 to 1939 were caused by payments for past, present, and future wars. "

Fiscal Year	Total Debt	Change	% Change
1937	$36,424,613,732.29		
1938	$37,164,740,315.15	$740,126,582.86	2.03%
1939	$40,439,532,411.11	$3,274,792,095.96	8.81%
1940	$42,967,531,037.68	$2,527,998,626.57	6.25%
1941	$48,961,443,535.71	$5,993,912,498.03	13.95%
Total		$12,536,829,803.42	34.42%

Now for the tally through 38 presidential terms and 32 Presidents.

Administration	Increased Debt	Decreased Debt	Party Totals
Democrat	8	5	13
Republican	6	7	13
Other	6	6	12
Total	20	18	38

President Franklin D. Roosevelt, a Democrat and our 32nd President, serving in the 39th presidential term. This administration began on 04 March 1941 running through 04 March 1945, encompassing the 77th and 78th Congresses. Both houses of both Congresses held Democratic majorities.

Here is yet another of my personal favorites from President Roosevelt:

"More than an end to war, we want an end to the beginning of all wars - yes, an end to this brutal, inhuman and thoroughly impractical method of settling the differences between governments."

Fiscal Year	Total Debt	Change	% Change
1941	$48,961,443,535.71		
1942	$72,422,445,116.22	$23,461,001,580.51	47.92%
1943	$136,696,090,329.90	$64,273,645,213.68	88.75%
1944	$201,003,387,221.13	$64,307,296,891.23	47.04%
1945	$258,682,187,409.93	$57,678,800,188.80	28.70%
Total		$209,720,743,874.22	428.34%

Now for the tally through 39 presidential terms and 32 Presidents.

Administration	Increased Debt	Decreased Debt	Party Totals
Democrat	9	5	14
Republican	6	7	13
Other	6	6	12
Total	21	18	39

President Franklin D. Roosevelt, a Democrat and our 32nd President, serving in the 40th presidential term. This administration began on 04 March 1945 and saw the death of President Roosevelt on 12 April 1945. President Harry S. Truman ascended the office becoming our 33rd President and completing this term through 20 January 1945, encompassing the 79th and 80th Congresses. The 79th was Democratic while the 80th was Republican.

One more from President Roosevelt:

"It is an unfortunate human failing that a full pocketbook often groans more loudly than an empty stomach."

President Truman is very quotable as well:

"My choice early in life was either to be a piano-player in a whorehouse or a politician. And to tell the truth, there's hardly any difference."

Fiscal Year	Total Debt	Change	% Change
1945	$258,682,187,409.93		
1946	$269,422,099,173.26	$10,739,911,763.33	4.15%
1947	$258,286,383,108.67	-$11,135,716,064.59	-4.13%
1948	$252,292,246,512.99	-$5,994,136,595.68	-2.32%
1949	$252,770,359,860.33	$478,113,347.34	0.19%
Total		-$5,911,827,549.60	-2.29%

Now for the tally through 40 presidential terms and 33 Presidents.

Administration	Increased Debt	Decreased Debt	Party Totals
Democrat	9	6	15
Republican	6	7	13
Other	6	6	12
Total	21	19	40

President Harry S. Truman, a Democrat and our 33rd President, serving in the 41st presidential term. Beginning on 20 January 1949 and running through 20 January 1953, encompassing the 81st and 82nd Congresses. Both Congresses were Democratic in both houses.

Another quote from President Truman:

"A pessimist is one who makes difficulties of his opportunities and an optimist is one who makes opportunities of his difficulties."

Fiscal Year	Total Debt	Change	% Change
1949	$252,770,359,860.33		
1950	$257,357,352,351.04	$4,586,992,490.71	1.81%
1951	$255,221,976,814.93	-$2,135,375,536.11	-0.83%
1952	$259,105,178,785.43	$3,883,201,970.50	1.52%
1953	$266,071,061,638.57	$6,965,882,853.14	2.69%
Total		$13,300,701,778.24	5.26%

Now for the tally through 41 presidential terms and 33 Presidents.

Administration	Increased Debt	Decreased Debt	Party Totals
Democrat	10	6	16
Republican	6	7	13
Other	6	6	12
Total	22	19	41

President Dwight D. Eisenhower, a Republican and our 34th President, serving in the 42nd presidential term. Beginning on 20 January 1953 and running through 20 January 1957, encompassing the 83rd and 84th Congresses. The 83rd had Democrats in both houses, while the 84th had Republicans in both houses.

One from President Eisenhower:

"An intellectual is a man who takes more words than necessary to tell more than he knows."

Fiscal Year	Total Debt	Change	% Change
1953	$266,071,061,638.57		
1954	$271,259,599,108.46	$5,188,537,469.89	1.95%
1955	$274,374,222,802.62	$3,114,623,694.16	1.15%
1956	$272,750,813,649.32	-$1,623,409,153.30	-0.59%
1957	$270,527,171,896.43	-$2,223,641,752.89	-0.82%
Total		$4,456,110,257.86	1.67%

Now for the tally through 42 presidential terms and 34 Presidents.

Administration	Increased Debt	Decreased Debt	Party Totals
Democrat	10	6	16
Republican	7	7	14
Other	6	6	12
Total	23	19	42

President Dwight D. Eisenhower, a Republican and our 34th President, serving in the 43rd presidential term. Beginning on 20 January 1957 and running through 20 January 1961, encompassing the 85th and 86th Congresses. Both houses of both Congresses were under Democratic majorities.

One more from President Eisenhower:

"Every gun that is made, every warship launched, every rocket fired, signifies in the final sense a theft from those who hunger and are not fed, those who are cold and are not clothed."

Fiscal Year	Total Debt	Change	% Change
1957	$270,527,171,896.43		
1958	$276,343,217,745.81	$5,816,045,849.38	2.15%
1959	$284,705,907,078.22	$8,362,689,332.41	3.03%
1960	$286,330,760,848.37	$1,624,853,770.15	0.57%
1961	$288,970,938,610.05	$2,640,177,761.68	0.92%
Total		$18,443,766,713.62	6.82%

Now for the tally through 43 presidential terms and 34 Presidents.

Administration	Increased Debt	Decreased Debt	Party Totals
Democrat	10	6	16
Republican	8	7	15
Other	6	6	12
Total	24	19	43

President John F. Kennedy, a Democrat and our 35th President, serving in the 44th presidential term. Beginning on 20 January 1961 and running to his death to an assassins bullets on 22 November 1963. President Lyndon B. Johnson ascended to the office becoming our 36th President and serving to the completion of this term on 20 January 1965. This term encompassed the 87th and 88th Congresses. Both houses of both Congresses enjoy Democratic majorities.

One of my favorite quotes from President Kennedy:

"A nation that is afraid to let its people judge the truth and falsehood in an open market is a nation that is afraid of its people."

Fiscal Year	Total Debt	Change	% Change
1961	$288,970,938,610.05		
1962	$298,200,822,720.87	$9,229,884,110.82	3.19%
1963	$305,859,632,996.41	$7,658,810,275.54	2.57%
1964	$311,712,899,257.30	$5,853,266,260.89	1.91%
1965	$317,273,898,983.64	$5,560,999,726.34	1.78%
Total		$28,302,960,373.59	9.79%

Now for the tally through 44 presidential terms and 36 Presidents.

Administration	Increased Debt	Decreased Debt	Party Totals
Democrat	11	6	17
Republican	8	7	15
Other	6	6	12
Total	25	19	44

President Lyndon B. Johnson, a Democrat and our 36th President, serving in the 45th presidential term, beginning on 20 January 1965 and runs through 20 January 1969. This term encompasses the 89th and 90th Congresses. Both houses of both Congresses held Democratic majorities.

A favorite from President Johnson:

"You do not examine legislation in the light of the benefits it will convey if properly administered, but in the light of the wrongs it would do and the harms it would cause if improperly administered."

Fiscal Year	Total Debt	Change	% Change
1965	$317,273,898,983.64		
1966	$319,907,087,795.48	$2,633,188,811.84	0.83%
1967	$326,220,937,794.54	$6,313,849,999.06	1.97%
1968	$347,578,406,425.88	$21,357,468,631.34	6.55%
1969	$353,720,253,841.41	$6,141,847,415.53	1.77%
Total		$36,446,354,857.77	11.49%

Now for the tally through 45 presidential terms and 36 Presidents.

Administration	Increased Debt	Decreased Debt	Party Totals
Democrat	12	6	18
Republican	8	7	15
Other	6	6	12
Total	26	19	45

President Richard M. Nixon, a Republican and our 37th President, serving in the 46th presidential term, beginning on 20 January 1969 and running through 20 January 1973. This term encompasses the 91st and 92nd Congresses. Both houses of both Congresses enjoyed Democratic majorities.

One from President Nixon.

"Never let your head hang down.
Never give up and sit down and grieve. Find another way.
And don't pray when it rains if you don't pray when the sun shines."

Fiscal Year	Total Debt	Change	% Change
1969	$353,720,253,841.41		
1970	$370,918,706,949.93	$17,198,453,108.52	4.86%
1971	$398,129,744,455.54	$27,211,037,505.61	7.34%
1972	$427,260,460,940.50	$29,130,716,484.96	7.32%
1973	$458,141,605,312.09	$30,881,144,371.59	7.23%
Total		$104,421,351,470.68	29.52%

Now for the tally through 46 presidential terms and 37 Presidents.

Administration	Increased Debt	Decreased Debt	Party Totals
Democrat	12	6	18
Republican	9	7	16
Other	6	6	12
Total	27	19	46

President Richard M. Nixon, a Republican and our 37th President, serving in the 47th presidential term, beginning on 20 January 1973 and serving through his resignation on 09 August 1974. President Gerald R. Ford ascended to the office becoming our 38th President and served the remainder of this term ending on 20 January 1977. This term encompasses the 93rd and 94th Congresses. Both houses have Democratic majorities in both houses.

Here's a quote from President Ford:

"A government big enough to give you everything you want is a government big enough to take from you everything you have."

Fiscal Year	Total Debt	Change	% Change
1973	$458,141,605,312.09		
1974	$475,059,815,731.55	$16,918,210,419.46	3.69%
1975	$533,189,000,000.00	$58,129,184,268.45	12.24%
1976	$620,433,000,000.00	$87,244,000,000.00	16.36%
1977	$698,840,000,000.00	$78,407,000,000.00	12.64%
Total		$240,698,394,687.91	52.54%

Now for the tally through 47 presidential terms and 38 Presidents.

Administration	Increased Debt	Decreased Debt	Party Totals
Democrat	12	6	18
Republican	10	7	17
Other	6	6	12
Total	28	19	47

There you have it. Our first 38 Presidents, presiding over 47 presidential terms. As you can see from the chart above the Democrats and the Republicans haven't performed nearly as well as the other administrations. The others are 50/50 on increasing vs. decreasing the national debt. The Republicans are next best at 41% decreasing and 59% increasing, followed by the Democrats at 33% decreasing and 67% increasing the debt.

As we move into what I consider to be the administrations of the modern age it will be interesting to see what transpires from here. If you remember when it all began for the constitutional United States government we finished our 1st fiscal year at $75,463,476.52. and we are, at this point in our story, up to $698,840,000,000.00, for an increase of $698,764,536,523.48. Just in case you were wondering that is an increase of 9,259%. While that seems like a lot, and it is, keep in mind that we are still well below the 1 trillion dollar mark, we haven't even made it to $700 billion just yet, and this was accumulated over 188 years a Revolutionary War, a Civil War, and 2 World Wars, not to mention the multitude of other conflicts in which our nation has been involved Lest we forget, landing a man on the moon.

This period was 188 years in length, so the average amount of increase per year was $3,716,832,641.08. As you will soon see, we are moving into a period for which borrowing this amount of money would be a slow week for the federal government of The United States of America, let alone a year.

Buckle up, I hope you have enjoyed the ride to this point, and I hope you are ready to talk about 13 and 14 digits on the left of the decimal point.

5 – JIMMY CARTER 1977 – 1981
(PRESIDENT 39 &
CONGRESSES 95 THROUGH 96)

"Elma Whitfeld's cousin Carlton went off to New York a normal boy, came back with his head shaved and an ear ring stuck in his cheek."

Brantly's dad

The Secret of my Success

President Jimmy Carter, a Democrat and our 39th President, serving in
the 48th presidential term. This administration began on 20 January 1977 and
ran through 20 January 1981. It encompassed the 95th and 96th Congresses.
Both houses of both Congresses were occupied by Democratic majorities.

To continue the little tradition we have established, here is one of my
favorite quotes from President Carter:

*"The best way to enhance freedom in other lands is to
demonstrate here that our democratic system is worthy of emulation."*

President Carter is often described as one of the worst Presidents but
one of the absolutely finest former Presidents due to his charitable works,
such as Habitat for Humanity. We are not here today to debate this issue
either way as it is far too subjective to be of use to anyone, if you remember,
our very narrow focus of this book is to evaluate the performance of each of
our administrations against their performance with regard to the national
debt, a very objective measure.

When President Carter took office in 1977 there were 11 cabinet level
departments. They were, State, Treasury, Defense, Attorney General,
Interior, Agriculture, Commerce, Labor, Health & Human Services,
Housing and Urban Development, and Transportation. The Carter
administration added two, Energy in 1978 and Education in 1979, moving
us to a total of 13.

Over the course of researching this book I have become very interested
in the rhetoric from our Presidents themselves, their speeches and press
conferences, more so once in office as opposed to the persona offered as
candidates. To that end for the remaining Presidents, beginning with this
one, we will read their inaugural addresses prior to examining their financial
stewardship.

Jimmy Carter, Inaugural Address, Thursday, 20 January, 1977

For myself and for our Nation, I want to thank my predecessor for
all he has done to heal our land.

In this outward and physical ceremony, we attest once again to the
inner and spiritual strength of our Nation. As my high school

teacher, Miss Julia Coleman, used to say, "We must adjust to changing times and still hold to unchanging principles."

Here before me is the Bible used in the inauguration of our first President, in 1789, and I have just taken the oath of office on the Bible my mother gave me just a few years ago, opened to a timeless admonition from the ancient prophet Micah: "He hath showed thee, O man, what is good; and what doth the Lord require of thee, but to do justly, and to love mercy, and to walk humbly with thy God."

This inauguration ceremony marks a new beginning, a new dedication within our Government, and a new spirit among us all. A President may sense and proclaim that new spirit, but only a people can provide it.

Two centuries ago, our Nation's birth was a milestone in the long quest for freedom. But the bold and brilliant dream which excited the founders of this Nation still awaits its consummation. I have no new dream to set forth today, but rather urge a fresh faith in the old dream.

Ours was the first society openly to define itself in terms of both spirituality and human liberty. It is that unique self-definition which has given us an exceptional appeal, but it also imposes on us a special obligation to take on those moral duties which, when assumed, seem invariably to be in our own best interests.

You have given me a great responsibility--to stay close to you, to be worthy of you, and to exemplify what you are. Let us create together a new national spirit of unity and trust. Your strength can compensate for my weakness, and your wisdom can help to minimize my mistakes.

Let us learn together and laugh together and work together and pray together, confident that in the end we will triumph together in the right.

The American dream endures. We must once again have full faith in our country--and in one another. I believe America can be better. We can be even stronger than before.

Let our recent mistakes bring a resurgent commitment to the basic principles of our Nation, for we know that if we despise our own government, we have no future. We recall in special times when we have stood briefly, but magnificently, united. In those times no prize was beyond our grasp.

But we cannot dwell upon remembered glory. We cannot afford to drift. We reject the prospect of failure or mediocrity or an inferior quality of life for any person. Our Government must at the same time be both competent and compassionate.

We have already found a high degree of personal liberty, and we are now struggling to enhance equality of opportunity. Our commitment to human rights must be absolute, our laws fair, our national beauty preserved; the powerful must not persecute the weak, and human dignity must be enhanced.

We have learned that more is not necessarily better, that even our great Nation has its recognized limits, and that we can neither answer all questions nor solve all problems. We cannot afford to do everything, nor can we afford to lack boldness as we meet the future. So, together, in a spirit of individual sacrifice for the common good, we must simply do our best.

Our Nation can be strong abroad only if it is strong at home. And we know that the best way to enhance freedom in other lands is to demonstrate here that our democratic system is worthy of emulation.

To be true to ourselves, we must be true to others. We will not behave in foreign places so as to violate our rules and standards here at home, for we know that the trust which our Nation earns is essential to our strength.

The world itself is now dominated by a new spirit. Peoples more numerous and more politically aware are craving, and now demanding, their place in the sun--not just for the benefit of their own physical condition, but for basic human rights.

The passion for freedom is on the rise. Tapping this new spirit, there can be no nobler nor more ambitious task for America to undertake on this day of a new beginning than to help shape a just and peaceful world that is truly humane.

We are a strong nation, and we will maintain strength so sufficient that it need not be proven in combat--a quiet strength based not merely on the size of an arsenal but on the nobility of ideas.

We will be ever vigilant and never vulnerable, and we will fight our wars against poverty, ignorance, and injustice, for those are the enemies against which our forces can be honorably marshaled.

We are a proudly idealistic nation, but let no one confuse our idealism with weakness.

Because we are free, we can never be indifferent to the fate of freedom elsewhere. Our moral sense dictates a clear-cut preference for those societies which share with us an abiding respect for individual human rights. We do not seek to intimidate, but it is clear that a world which others can dominate with impunity would be inhospitable to decency and a threat to the well-being of all people.

The world is still engaged in a massive armaments race designed to ensure continuing equivalent strength among potential adversaries. We pledge perseverance and wisdom in our efforts to limit the world's armaments to those necessary for each nation's own domestic safety. And we will move this year a step toward our ultimate goal--the elimination of all nuclear weapons from this Earth. We urge all other people to join us, for success can mean life instead of death.

Within us, the people of the United States, there is evident a serious and purposeful rekindling of confidence. And I join in the hope that when my time as your President has ended, people might say this about our nation:

--that we had remembered the words of Micah and renewed our search for humility, mercy, and justice; --that we had torn down the barriers that separated those of different race and region and religion, and where there had been mistrust, built unity, with a respect for diversity; --that we had found productive work for those able to perform it; --that we had strengthened the American family, which is the basis of our society; --that we had ensured respect for the law and equal treatment under the law, for the weak and the powerful, for the rich and the poor; and --that we had enabled our people to be proud of their own Government once again.

I would hope that the nations of the world might say that we had built a lasting peace, based not on weapons of war but on international policies which reflect our own most precious values.

These are not just my goals---and they will not be my accomplishments-but the affirmation of our Nation's continuing moral strength and our belief in an undiminished, ever-expanding American dream.

Thank you very much

Jimmy Carter, Inaugural Address, Thursday, 20 January, 1977

As you have no doubt noticed there was no mention of the state of the finances of The United States, as related to the national debt, in the inaugural address of President Carter. Further, while not included here the platform of the Democratic Party from 1976 mentions deficits only in passing.

As we prepare to reveal the results for this administration, it bears remembering that the per year average increase to the national debt for the 188 year history of the constitutional United States

government leading up to the inauguration of President Carter was
$3,716,832,641.08.

If you are ready, lets turn the page and get the verdict on our
39th President and the 48th presidential term.

Fiscal Year	Total Debt	Change	% Change
1977	$698,840,000,000.00		
1978	$771,544,000,000.00	$72,704,000,000.00	10.40%
1979	$826,519,000,000.00	$54,975,000,000.00	7.13%
1980	$907,701,000,000.00	$81,182,000,000.00	9.82%
1981	$997,855,000,000.00	$90,154,000,000.00	9.93%
Total		$299,015,000,000.00	42.79%

There you have it. The per year average increase for this administration
was an increase of $74,753,750,000.00 to the national debt. Over the course
of this 4 year term the national debt was increased by 42.79%. Almost half as
much was added in a single 4 year term as had been accumulated in the
previous 188 years.

At this point we are going to begin keeping track of our per year
average increase to the national debt for each administration and it's affect
on the per year average for the history of our constitutional form of
government. I believe this information is most effectively conveyed in the
form of a table and therefore we are going to add one more to our usual 2.
The first will always reflect the total number of years up to the beginning of
the administration under consideration. The second will reflect the number
of years total to the end of the administration under consideration.

Years of Existence	Total Debt	Total Change	Per Year Average Increase
1	$75,463,476.52		
188	$698,840,000,000.00	$698,764,536,523.48	$3,716,832,641.08
192	$997,855,000,000.00	$997,779,536,523.48	$5,197,161,458.33
	Percentage Change In	The per year Average	39.83%

This administration increased the average per year amount of increase to the national debt by 39.83%.

Now for the tally through 48 presidential terms and 39 Presidents.

Administration	Increased Debt	Decreased Debt	Party Totals
Democrat	13	6	19
Republican	10	7	17
Other	6	6	12
Total	29	19	48

Now the numbers from the Democratic administration of President Carter are huge. However if you are thinking this is a poor performance, well lets just say you might want to hold onto your hat, and every other article of clothing, as we move forward. If these guys and girls were incompetent amateurs, when it comes to borrowing money at least, then get ready to meet the thoroughly competent professionals.

6 – RONALD REAGAN 1981 – 1989
(PRESIDENT 40 &
CONGRESSES 97 THROUGH 100)

"Ehhhh it's my brother's house, he'll take care of it. "

Frank McCallister

Home Alone

President Ronald Reagan, a Republican and our 40th President, serving in the 49th presidential term. This administration began on 20 January 1981 and ran through 20 January 1985. It encompassed the 97th and 98th Congresses. These 2 Congresses shared similar majorities with Republicans in the Senate and Democrats in the House.

A humorous one from President Reagan:

"I am not worried about the deficit.
It is big enough to take care of itself."

President Reagan is largely regarded as one of our finest Presidents, again as with President Carter, we are not here to argue that point. Our purpose is to objectively measure performance against the national debt. As with President Carter we will begin by reading President Reagan's inaugural address.

Ronald Reagan, Inaugural Address, 20 January 1981

Senator Hatfield, Mr. Chief Justice, Mr. President, Vice President Bush, Vice President Mondale, Senator Baker, Speaker O'Neill, Reverend Moomaw, and my fellow citizens:

To a few of us here today this is a solemn and most momentous occasion, and yet in the history of our nation it is a commonplace occurrence. The orderly transfer of authority as called for in the Constitution routinely takes place, as it has for almost two centuries, and few of us stop to think how unique we really are. In the eyes of many in the world, this every 4-year ceremony we accept as normal is nothing less than a miracle.

Mr. President, I want our fellow citizens to know how much you did to carry on this tradition. By your gracious cooperation in the transition process, you have shown a watching world that we are a united people pledged to maintaining a political system which guarantees individual liberty to a greater degree than any other, and I thank you and your people for all your help in maintaining the continuity which is the bulwark of our Republic.

The business of our nation goes forward. These United States are confronted with an economic affliction of great proportions. We suffer from the longest and one of the worst sustained inflations in our national history. It distorts our economic decisions, penalizes thrift, and crushes the struggling young and the fixed-income elderly alike. It threatens to shatter the lives of millions of our people.

Idle industries have cast workers into unemployment, human misery, and personal indignity. Those who do work are denied a fair return for their labor by a tax system which penalizes successful achievement and keeps us from maintaining full productivity.

But great as our tax burden is, it has not kept pace with public spending. For decades we have piled deficit upon deficit, mortgaging our future and our children's future for the temporary convenience of the present. To continue this long trend is to guarantee tremendous social, cultural, political, and economic upheavals.

You and I, as individuals, can, by borrowing, live beyond our means, but for only a limited period of time. Why, then, should we think that collectively, as a nation, we're not bound by that same limitation? We must act today in order to preserve tomorrow. And let there be no misunderstanding: We are going to begin to act, beginning today.

The economic ills we suffer have come upon us over several decades. They will not go away in days, weeks, or months, but they will go away. They will go away because we as Americans have the capacity now, as we've had in the past, to do whatever needs to be done to preserve this last and greatest bastion of freedom.

In this present crisis, government is not the solution to our problem; government is the problem. From time to time we've been tempted to believe that society has become too complex to be managed by self-rule, that government by an elite group is superior to government for, by, and of the people. Well, if no one among us is capable of governing himself, then who among us has the capacity to govern someone else? All of us together, in and out of government, must bear the burden. The solutions we seek must be equitable, with no one group singled out to pay a higher price.

We hear much of special interest groups. Well, our concern must be for a special interest group that has been too long neglected. It knows no sectional boundaries or ethnic and racial divisions, and it crosses political party lines. It is made up of men and women who raise our food, patrol our streets, man our mines and factories, teach our children, keep our homes, and heal us when we're sick—professionals, industrialists, shopkeepers, clerks, cabbies, and truck drivers. They are, in short, "We the people," this breed called Americans.

Well, this administration's objective will be a healthy, vigorous, growing economy that provides equal opportunities for all Americans, with no barriers born of bigotry or discrimination. Putting America back to work means putting all Americans back to work. Ending inflation means freeing all Americans from the terror of runaway living costs. All must share in the productive work of this "new beginning," and all must share in the bounty of a revived economy. With the idealism and fair play which are the core of our system and our strength, we can have a strong and prosperous America, at peace with itself and the world.

So, as we begin, let us take inventory. We are a nation that has a government—not the other way around. And this makes us special among the nations of the Earth. Our government has no power except that granted it by the people. It is time to check and reverse the growth of government, which shows signs of having grown beyond the consent of the governed.

It is my intention to curb the size and influence of the Federal establishment and to demand recognition of the distinction between the powers granted to the Federal Government and those reserved to the States or to the people. All of us need to be reminded that the Federal Government did not create the States; the States created the Federal Government.

Now, so there will be no misunderstanding, it's not my intention to do away with government. It is rather to make it work--work with us, not over us; to stand by our side, not ride on our back. Government can and must provide opportunity, not smother it; foster productivity, not stifle it.

If we look to the answer as to why for so many years we achieved so much, prospered as no other people on Earth, it was because here in this land we unleashed the energy and individual genius of man to a greater extent than has ever been done before. Freedom and the dignity of the individual have been more available and assured here than in any other place on Earth. The price for this freedom at times has been high, but we have never been unwilling to pay that price.

It is no coincidence that our present troubles parallel and are proportionate to the intervention and intrusion in our lives that result from unnecessary and excessive growth of government. It is time for us to realize that we're too great a nation to limit ourselves to small dreams. We're not, as some would have us believe, doomed to an inevitable decline. I do not believe in a fate that will fall on us no matter what we do. I do believe in a fate that will fall on us if we do nothing. So, with all the creative energy at our command, let us begin an era of national renewal. Let us renew our determination, our courage, and our strength. And let us renew our faith and our hope.

We have every right to dream heroic dreams. Those who say that we're in a time when there are not heroes, they just don't know where to look. You can see heroes every day going in and out of factory gates. Others, a handful in number, produce enough food to feed all of us and then the world beyond. You meet heroes across a counter, and they're on both sides of that counter. There are entrepreneurs with faith in themselves and faith in an idea who create new jobs, new wealth and opportunity. They're individuals and families whose taxes support the government and whose voluntary gifts support church, charity, culture, art, and education.

Their patriotism is quiet, but deep. Their values sustain our national life.

Now, I have used the words "they" and "their" in speaking of these heroes. I could say "you" and "your," because I'm addressing the heroes of whom I speak—you, the citizens of this blessed land. Your dreams, your hopes, your goals are going to be the dreams, the hopes, and the goals of this administration, so help me God.

We shall reflect the compassion that is so much a part of your makeup. How can we love our country and not love our countrymen; and loving them, reach out a hand when they fall, heal them when they're sick, and provide opportunity to make them self-sufficient so they will be equal in fact and not just in theory?

Can we solve the problems confronting us? Well, the answer is an unequivocal and emphatic "yes." To paraphrase Winston Churchill, I did not take the oath I've just taken with the intention of presiding over the dissolution of the world's strongest economy.

In the days ahead I will propose removing the roadblocks that have slowed our economy and reduced productivity. Steps will be taken aimed at restoring the balance between the various levels of government. Progress may be slow, measured in inches and feet, not miles, but we will progress. It is time to reawaken this industrial giant, to get government back within its means, and to lighten our punitive tax burden. And these will be our first priorities, and on these principles there will be no compromise.

On the eve of our struggle for independence a man who might have been one of the greatest among the Founding Fathers, Dr. Joseph Warren, President of the Massachusetts Congress, said to his fellow Americans, "Our country is in danger, but not to be despaired of . . . . On you depend the fortunes of America. You are to decide the important questions upon which rests the happiness and the liberty of millions yet unborn. Act worthy of yourselves."

Well, I believe we, the Americans of today, are ready to act worthy of ourselves, ready to do what must be done to ensure happiness and liberty for ourselves, our children, and our children's children. And as we renew ourselves here in our own land, we will be seen as having greater strength throughout the world. We will again be the exemplar of freedom and a beacon of hope for those who do not now have freedom.

To those neighbors and allies who share our freedom, we will strengthen our historic ties and assure them of our support and firm commitment. We will match loyalty with loyalty. We will strive for mutually beneficial relations. We will not use our friendship to impose on their sovereignty, for our own sovereignty is not for sale.

As for the enemies of freedom, those who are potential adversaries, they will be reminded that peace is the highest aspiration of the American people. We will negotiate for it, sacrifice for it; we will not surrender for it, now or ever.

Our forbearance should never be misunderstood. Our reluctance for conflict should not be misjudged as a failure of will. When action is required to preserve our national security, we will act. We will maintain sufficient strength to prevail if need be, knowing that if we do so we have the best chance of never having to use that strength.

Above all, we must realize that no arsenal or no weapon in the arsenals of the world is so formidable as the will and moral courage of free men and women. It is a weapon our adversaries in today's world do not have. It is a weapon that we as Americans do have. Let that be understood by those who practice terrorism and prey upon their neighbors.

I'm told that tens of thousands of prayer meetings are being held on this day, and for that I'm deeply grateful. We are a nation under God, and I believe God intended for us to be free. It would be fitting and good, I think, if on each Inaugural Day in future years it should be declared a day of prayer.

This is the first time in our history that this ceremony has been held, as you've been told, on this West Front of the Capitol. Standing here, one faces a magnificent vista, opening up on this city's special beauty and history. At the end of this open mall are those shrines to the giants on whose shoulders we stand.

Directly in front of me, the monument to a monumental man, George Washington, father of our country. A man of humility who came to greatness reluctantly. He led America out of revolutionary victory into infant nationhood. Off to one side, the stately memorial to Thomas Jefferson. The Declaration of Independence flames with his eloquence. And then, beyond the Reflecting Pool, the dignified columns of the Lincoln Memorial. Whoever would understand in his heart the meaning of America will find it in the life of Abraham Lincoln.

Beyond those monuments to heroism is the Potomac River, and on the far shore the sloping hills of Arlington National Cemetery, with its row upon row of simple white markers bearing crosses or Stars of David. They add up to only a tiny fraction of the price that has been paid for our freedom.

Each one of those markers is a monument to the kind of hero I spoke of earlier. Their lives ended in places called Belleau Wood, The Argonne, Omaha Beach, Salerno, and halfway around the world on Guadalcanal, Tarawa, Pork Chop Hill, the Chosin Reservoir, and in a hundred rice paddies and jungles of a place called Vietnam.

Under one such marker lies a young man, Martin Treptow, who left his job in a small town barbershop in 1917 to go to France with the famed Rainbow Division. There, on the western front, he was killed trying to carry a message between battalions under heavy artillery fire.

We're told that on his body was found a diary. On the flyleaf under the heading, "My Pledge," he had written these words: "America must win this war. Therefore I will work, I will save, I will sacrifice,

I will endure, I will fight cheerfully and do my utmost, as if the issue of the whole struggle depended on me alone."

The crisis we are facing today does not require of us the kind of sacrifice that Martin Treptow and so many thousands of others were called upon to make. It does require, however, our best effort and our willingness to believe in ourselves and to believe in our capacity to perform great deeds, to believe that together with God's help we can and will resolve the problems which now confront us.

And after all, why shouldn't we believe that? We are Americans. God bless you, and thank you.

Ronald Reagan, Inaugural Address, 20 January 1981

Unlike President Carter, President Reagan acknowledged the national debt and spoke of the necessity of gaining control over it. Paragraphs 6 and 7 of this address speak directly to the need for fiscal responsibility and further proclaims that it has arrived with the beginning of this administration. These 2 paragraphs are excerpted and reprinted here for clarity.

"But great as our tax burden is, it has not kept pace with public spending. For decades we have piled deficit upon deficit, mortgaging our future and our children's future for the temporary convenience of the present. To continue this long trend is to guarantee tremendous social, cultural, political, and economic upheavals.

You and I, as individuals, can, by borrowing, live beyond our means, but for only a limited period of time. Why, then, should we think that collectively, as a nation, we're not bound by that same limitation? We must act today in order to preserve tomorrow. And let there be no misunderstanding: We are going to begin to act, beginning today."

A pretty direct statement don't you think. The expectation has been set by the President himself on the occasion of his first official act, the delivery of his first inaugural address. It seems very clear that he has a great concern for the level of debt he is inheriting as well as the very obvious trend of adding to it, quite generously, year after year.

Future President George H. W. Bush has a quote that has become quite famous or infamous, depending on your point of view. Does anyone else remember this, *"Read My Lips, No New Taxes"*? Well lets turn the page and find out if President Reagan's legacy should include the following,

"And let there be no misunderstanding:
We are going to begin to act, beginning today."

Fiscal Year	Total Debt	Change	% Change
1981	$997,855,000,000.00		
1982	$1,142,034,000,000.00	$144,179,000,000.00	14.45%
1983	$1,377,210,000,000.00	$235,176,000,000.00	20.59%
1984	$1,572,266,000,000.00	$195,056,000,000.00	14.16%
1985	$1,823,103,000,000.00	$250,837,000,000.00	15.95%
Total		$825,248,000,000.00	82.70%

Well, we most certainly did begin to act it would appear. As you can see from the table above this administration increased the national debt by nearly 83% in just 4 years. This massive, mammoth, monstrous, mega... where is the thesaurus when you need one, increase on the heels of an inaugural address stressing not only the need for redirect but the suggestion that not doing so would be the height of ir-responsibility. Are you beginning to loose faith a little bit? I know all of this is very discouraging, but hang in there, it really isn't hopeless. At least I don't think it is.

Let's take a look at our new chart to see how the average increase is fairing as we add these "modern" administrations to the mix.

Years of Existence	Total Debt	Total Change	Per Year Average Increase
1	$75,463,476.52		
192	$997,855,000,000.00	$997,779,536,523.48	$5,197,161,458.33
196	$1,823,103,000,000.00	$825,248,000,000.00	$9,301,545,918.37
	Percentage Change In	The per year Average	78.97%

Well, after these 4 years the average increase per year since inception of the constitutional government has nearly doubled to over 9 billion annually. Now for the tally through 49 presidential terms and 40 Presidents.

Administration	Increased Debt	Decreased Debt	Party Totals
Democrat	13	6	19
Republican	11	7	18
Other	6	6	12
Total	30	19	49

As you can see, there isn't a heck of a lot of difference in the performance of the parties so far and it's getting still closer with every administration we add.

Beginning on the very next page we will examine the 2nd of 2 terms for President Reagan. I feel it safe to say this one was a massive, mammoth, monstrous, mega...., I know you have seen this before, failure on the promises made regarding the national debt in the inaugural address. But perhaps we are just not looking at it from the correct point of view. I offer the following snippet, also from President Reagan's first inaugural as evidence.:

"For decades we have piled deficit upon deficit, mortgaging our future and our children's future for the temporary convenience of the present."

followed shortly by:

"You and I, as individuals, can, by borrowing, live beyond our means"

Perhaps this administration gave us exactly what was promised after all. Now, obviously, these 2 phrases are out of context. We are just having a little fun here. Remember an earlier warning: "You are going to need your sense of humor!"

Let's move on and see what he had to say in his 2nd inaugural and more importantly the condition of the debt at it's end.

Charles F. Stamper

President Ronald Reagan, a Republican and our 40th President, serving in the 50th presidential term. This administration began on 20 January 1985 and ran through 20 January 1989. It encompassed the 99th and 100th Congresses. The 99th Congress is split with Republicans in the senate and Democrats in the house, while the 100th has Democrats in both chambers.

This is the 2nd of 2 terms for President Reagan, so without further adieu, lets take a look at the 2nd inaugural address.

Ronald Reagan, Inaugural Address, 21 January 1985

Senator Mathias, Chief Justice Burger, Vice President Bush, Speaker O'Neill, Senator Dole, reverend clergy, and members of my family and friends and my fellow citizens:

This day has been made brighter with the presence here of one who, for a time, has been absent. Senator John Stennis, God bless you and welcome back.

There is, however, one who is not with us today. Representative Gillis Long of Louisiana left us last night. And I wonder if we could all join in a moment of silent prayer.

[The President resumed speaking after a moment of silence.]

Amen.

There are no words adequate to express my thanks for the great honor that you've bestowed on me. I'll do my utmost to be deserving of your trust.

This is, as Senator Mathias told us, the 50th time that we, the people, have celebrated this historic occasion. When the first President, George Washington, placed his hand upon the Bible, he stood less than a single day's journey by horseback from raw, untamed wilderness. There were 4 million Americans in a union of 13 States. Today, we are 60 times as many in a union of 50 States. We've lighted the world with our inventions, gone to the aid of mankind wherever in the world there was a cry for help, journeyed to the Moon and safely returned. So much has changed, and yet we stand together as we did two centuries ago.

When I took this oath 4 years ago, I did so in a time of economic stress. Voices were raised saying that we had to look to our past for the greatness and glory. But we, the present-day Americans, are not given to looking backward. In this blessed land, there is always a better tomorrow.

Four years ago, I spoke to you of a New Beginning, and we have accomplished that. But in another sense, our New Beginning is a continuation of that beginning created two centuries ago when, for the first time in history, government, the people said, was not our master, it is our servant; its only power that which we the people allow it to have.

That system has never failed us, but for a time we failed the system. We asked things of government that government was not equipped to give. We yielded authority to the National Government that properly belonged to States or to local governments or to the people themselves. We allowed taxes and inflation to rob us of our earnings and savings and watched the great industrial machine that had made us the most productive people on Earth slow down and the number of unemployed increase.

By 1980 we knew it was time to renew our faith, to strive with all our strength toward the ultimate in individual freedom, consistent with an orderly society.

We believed then and now: There are no limits to growth and human progress when men and women are free to follow their dreams. And we were right to believe that. Tax rates have been reduced, inflation cut dramatically, and more people are employed than ever before in our history.

We are creating a nation once again vibrant, robust, and alive. But there are many mountains yet to climb. We will not rest until every

American enjoys the fullness of freedom, dignity, and opportunity as our birthright. It is our birthright as citizens of this great Republic.

And if we meet this challenge, these will be years when Americans have restored their confidence and tradition of progress; when our values of faith, family, work, and neighborhood were restated for a modern age; when our economy was finally freed from government's grip; when we made sincere efforts at meaningful arms reductions and by rebuilding our defenses, our economy, and developing new technologies, helped preserve peace in a troubled world; when America courageously supported the struggle for individual liberty, self-government, and free enterprise throughout the world and turned the tide of history away from totalitarian darkness and into the warm sunlight of human freedom.

My fellow citizens, our nation is poised for greatness. We must do what we know is right, and do it with all our might. Let history say of us: "These were golden years-when the American Revolution was reborn, when freedom gained new life, and America reached for her best.

Our two-party system has solved us-served us, I should say, well over the years, but never better than in those times of great challenge when we came together not as Democrats or Republicans, but as Americans united in a common cause.

Two of our Founding Fathers, a Boston lawyer named Adams and a Virginia planter named Jefferson, members of that remarkable group who met in Independence Hall and dared to think they could start the world over again, left us an important lesson. They had become, in the years then in government, bitter political rivals in the Presidential election of 1800. Then, years later, when both were retired and age had softened their anger, they began to speak to each other again through letters. A bond was reestablished between those two who had helped create this government of ours.

In 1826, the 50th anniversary of the Declaration of Independence, they both died. They died on the same day, within a few hours of each other, and that day was the Fourth of July.

In one of those letters exchanged in the sunset of their lives, Jefferson wrote: "It carries me back to the times when, beset with difficulties and dangers, we were fellow laborers in the same cause, struggling for what is most valuable to man, his right of self-government. Laboring always at the same oar, with some wave ever ahead threatening to overwhelm us, and yet passing harmless... we rode through the storm with heart and hand."

Well, with heart and hand let us stand as one today—one people under God, determined that our future shall be worthy of our past. As we do, we must not repeat the well-intentioned errors of our past. We must never again abuse the trust of working men and women by sending their earnings on a futile chase after the spiraling demands of a bloated Federal Establishment. You elected us in 1980 to end this prescription for disaster, and I don't believe you reelected us in 1984 to reverse course.

At the heart of our efforts is one idea vindicated by 25 straight months of economic growth: Freedom and incentives unleash the drive and entrepreneurial genius that are the core of human progress. We have begun to increase the rewards for work, savings, and investment; reduce the increase in the cost and size of government and its interference in people's lives.

We must simplify our tax system, make it more fair and bring the rates down for all who work and earn. We must think anew and move with a new boldness, so every American who seeks work can find work, so the least among us shall have an equal chance to achieve the greatest things—to be heroes who heal our sick, feed the hungry, protect peace among nations, and leave this world a better place.

The time has come for a new American emancipation—a great national drive to tear down economic barriers and liberate the spirit of enterprise in the most distressed areas of our country. My friends, together we can do this, and do it we must, so help me God.

From new freedom will spring new opportunities for growth, a more productive, fulfilled, and united people, and a stronger America—an America that will lead the technological revolution and also open its mind and heart and soul to the treasures of literature, music, and poetry, and the values of faith, courage, and love.

A dynamic economy, with more citizens working and paying taxes, will be our strongest tool to bring down budget deficits. But an almost unbroken 50 years of deficit spending has finally brought us to a time of reckoning. We've come to a turning point, a moment for hard decisions. I have asked the Cabinet and my staff a question and now I put the same question to all of you. If not us, who? And if not now, when? It must be done by all of us going forward with a program aimed at reaching a balanced budget. We can then begin reducing the national debt.

I will shortly submit a budget to the Congress aimed at freezing government program spending for the next year. Beyond this, we must take further steps to permanently control government's power to tax and spend. We must act now to protect future generations from government's desire to spend its citizens' money and tax them into servitude when the bills come due. Let us make it unconstitutional for the Federal Government to spend more than the Federal Government takes in.

We have already started returning to the people and to State and local governments responsibilities better handled by them. Now, there is a place for the Federal Government in matters of social compassion. But our fundamental goals must be to reduce dependency and upgrade the dignity of those who are infirm or disadvantaged. And here, a growing economy and support from family and community offer our best chance for a society where compassion is a way of life, where the old and infirm are cared for, the young and, yes, the unborn protected, and the unfortunate looked after and made self-sufficient.

Now, there is another area where the Federal Government can play a part. As an older American, I remember a time when people of different race, creed, or ethnic origin in our land found hatred and prejudice installed in social custom and, yes, in law. There's no story more heartening in our history than the progress that we've made toward the brotherhood of man that God intended for us. Let us resolve there will be no turning back or hesitation on the road to an America rich in dignity and abundant with opportunity for all our citizens.

Let us resolve that we, the people, will build an American opportunity society in which all of us—white and black, rich and poor, young and old—will go forward together, arm in arm. Again, let us remember that though our heritage is one of blood lines from every corner of the Earth, we are all Americans, pledged to carry on this last, best hope of man on Earth.

I've spoken of our domestic goals and the limitations we should put on our National Government. Now let me turn to a task that is the primary responsibility of National Government—the safety and security of our people.

Today, we utter no prayer more fervently than the ancient prayer for peace on Earth. Yet history has shown that peace does not come, nor will our freedom be preserved, by good will alone. There are those in the world who scorn our vision of human dignity and freedom. One nation, the Soviet Union, has conducted the greatest military buildup in the history of man, building arsenals of awesome offensive weapons.

We've made progress in restoring our defense capability. But much remains to be done. There must be no wavering by us, nor any doubts by others, that America will meet her responsibilities to remain free, secure, and at peace.

There is only one way safely and legitimately to reduce the cost of national security, and that is to reduce the need for it. And this we're trying to do in negotiations with the Soviet Union. We're not just discussing limits on a further increase of nuclear weapons; we seek, instead, to reduce their number. We seek the total elimination one day of nuclear weapons from the face of the Earth.

Now, for decades, we and the Soviets have lived under the threat of mutual assured destruction—if either resorted to the use of nuclear weapons, the other could retaliate and destroy the one who had started it. Is there either logic or morality in believing that if one side threatens to kill tens of millions of our people our only recourse is to threaten killing tens of millions of theirs?

I have approved a research program to find, if we can, a security shield that will destroy nuclear missiles before they reach their target. It wouldn't kill people; it would destroy weapons. It wouldn't militarize space; it would help demilitarize the arsenals of Earth. It would render nuclear weapons obsolete. We will meet with the Soviets, hoping that we can agree on a way to rid the world of the threat of nuclear destruction.

We strive for peace and security, heartened by the changes all around us. Since the turn of the century, the number of democracies in the world has grown fourfold. Human freedom is on the march, and nowhere more so than in our own hemisphere. Freedom is one of the deepest and noblest aspirations of the human spirit. People, worldwide, hunger for the right of self-determination, for those inalienable rights that make for human dignity and progress.

America must remain freedom's staunchest friend, for freedom is our best ally and it is the world's only hope to conquer poverty and preserve peace. Every blow we inflict against poverty will be a blow against its dark allies of oppression and war. Every victory for human freedom will be a victory for world peace.

So, we go forward today, a nation still mighty in its youth and powerful in its purpose. With our alliances strengthened, with our economy leading the world to a new age of economic expansion, we look to a future rich in possibilities. And all of this is because we worked and acted together, not as members of political parties but as Americans.

My friends, we live in a world that's lit by lightning. So much is changing and will change, but so much endures and transcends time.

History is a ribbon, always unfurling. History is a journey. And as we continue our journey, we think of those who traveled before us. We stand again at the steps of this symbol of our democracy—well, we would have been standing at the steps if it hadn't gotten so cold. [Laughter] Now we're standing inside this symbol of our democracy, and we see and hear again the echoes of our past: a general falls to his knees in the hard snow of Valley Forge; a lonely President paces the darkened halls and ponders his struggle to preserve the Union; the men of the Alamo call out encouragement to each other; a settler pushes west and sings a song, and the song echoes out forever and fills the unknowing air.

It is the American sound. It is hopeful, big-hearted, idealistic, daring, decent, and fair. That's our heritage, that's our song. We sing it still. For all our problems, our differences, we are together as of old. We raise our voices to the God who is the Author of this most tender music. And may He continue to hold us close as we fill the world with our sound—in unity, affection, and love—one people under God, dedicated to the dream of freedom that He has placed in the human heart, called upon now to pass that dream on to a waiting and hopeful world.

God bless you, and God bless America

Ronald Reagan, Inaugural Address, 21 January 1985

Here is a snippet from this address that once again speaks to the necessity to reign in the spiraling national debt:

"A dynamic economy, with more citizens working and paying taxes, will be our strongest tool to bring down budget deficits. But an almost unbroken 50 years of deficit spending has finally brought us to a time of reckoning. We've come to a turning point, a moment for hard decisions. I have asked the Cabinet and my staff a question and now I put the same

question to all of you. If not us, who? And if not now, when? It must be done by all of us going forward with a program aimed at reaching a balanced budget. We can then begin reducing the national debt."

What to say, what to say. It's almost as if he were asleep for the past 4 years. His first administration increased the national debt accumulated over 192 years preceding him by a whopping 83%. Yet the text of this speech reads as though there were a new renaissance in the financial condition of this country. Remember way back in the prologue I shared my feeling that listening to modern politicians left me with a feeling that something was not quite accurate. Well welcome to a huge case in point.

We have been prepared once again, the expectation has been set by the President himself. On the measure of responsible treatment of the national debt, I feel it fair to say that the first administration didn't live up to it's promises. Let's see how this one performed.

Fiscal Year	Total Debt	Change	% Change
1985	$1,823,103,000,000.00		
1986	$2,125,302,616,658.42	$302,199,616,658.42	16.58%
1987	$2,350,276,890,953.00	$224,974,274,294.58	10.59%
1988	$2,602,337,712,041.16	$252,060,821,088.16	10.72%
1989	$2,857,430,960,187.32	$255,093,248,146.16	9.80%
Total		$1,034,327,960,187.32	56.73%

Well now, another increase of 56%. Keep in mind that this increase is on top of the 82% increase from the first term. When President Reagan took office in 1981 the national debt stood at $997,855,000,000.00, when he left office in 1989 it stood at $2,857,430,960,187.32 for an increase of $1,859,575,960,187.32. That is an increase of 186% in 8 years. In other words these 2 administrations have added very nearly twice as much to the national debt in 8 years as had been accumulated in the 192 years preceding them.

That is why the preceding chapter ended with an invitation to meet the "competent professionals". Now we are going to take a look at our chart tracking the per year average increase to the national debt.

Years of Existenc e	Total Debt	Total Change	Per Year Average Increase
1	$75,463,476.52		
196	$1,823,103,000,000.00	$1,823,027,536,523.48	$9,301,545,918.37
200	$2,857,430,960,187.32	$1,034,327,960,187.32	$14,287,154,800.94
	Percentage Change In	The per year Average	53.60%

After adding just 3 of what I have defined as the modern administrations to this chart we find that our average annual addition to the national debt since inception of our constitutional government has be driven up to $14,287,154,800.94. It bears repeating that at the end of the administration of President Ford the average annual increase stood at $3,716,832,641.08. that is an increase of 384% on the average rate of change to the national debt after adding 12 years to the first 188 years.

Now for the tally through 50 presidential terms and 40 Presidents.

Administration	Increased Debt	Decreased Debt	Party Totals
Democrat	13	6	19
Republican	12	7	19
Other	6	6	12
Total	31	19	50

In other words, "Ehhh, It's my brothers house. He'll take care of it."

7 – GEORGE H. W. BUSH 1989 – 1993 (PRESIDENT 41 & CONGRESSES 101 THROUGH 102)

"Option B is pretty much the opposite of option A. But I wouldn't recommend it!"

Beck

The Rundown

President George H. W. Bush, a Republican and our 41st President, serving in the 51st presidential term. This administration began on 20 January 1989 and ran through 20 January 1993. It encompassed the 101st and 102nd Congresses. Both houses of both Congresses held Democratic majorities in both chambers.

President H. W. Bush doesn't seem to stir emotions in people as did his predecessor or President Clinton who will follow him in the office. He is probably remembered most for a promise he made while campaigning, referenced in the preceding chapter, "Read my lips. No new taxes". Lets take this opportunity to read his inaugural address and then we will chart the results of this administrations performance as it relates to the national debt.

President George H. W. Bush, Inaugural Address, 20 January 1989

Mr. Chief Justice, Mr. President, Vice President Quayle, Senator Mitchell, Speaker Wright, Senator Dole, Congressman Michel, and fellow citizens, neighbors, and friends:

There is a man here who has earned a lasting place in our hearts and in our history. President Reagan, on behalf of our nation, I thank you for the wonderful things that you have done for America.

I've just repeated word for word the oath taken by George Washington 200 years ago, and the Bible on which I placed my hand is the Bible on which he placed his. It is right that the memory of Washington be with us today not only because this is our bicentennial inauguration but because Washington remains the Father of our Country. And he would, I think, be gladdened by this day; for today is the concrete expression of a stunning fact: our continuity, these 200 years, since our government began.

We meet on democracy's front porch. A good place to talk as neighbors and as friends. For this is a day when our nation is made whole, when our differences, for a moment, are suspended. And my first act as President is a prayer. I ask you to bow your heads.

Heavenly Father, we bow our heads and thank You for Your love. Accept our thanks for the peace that yields this day and the shared faith that makes its continuance likely. Make us strong to do Your work, willing to heed and hear Your will, and write on our hearts these words: "Use power to help people." For we are given power not to advance our own purposes, nor to make a great show in the world, nor a name. There is but one just use of power, and it is to serve people. Help us remember, Lord. Amen.

I come before you and assume the Presidency at a moment rich with promise. We live in a peaceful, prosperous time, but we can make it better. For a new breeze is blowing, and a world refreshed by freedom seems reborn. For in man's heart, if not in fact, the day of the dictator is over. The totalitarian era is passing, its old ideas blown away like leaves from an ancient, lifeless tree. A new breeze is blowing, and a nation refreshed by freedom stands ready to push on. There is new ground to be broken and new action to be taken. There are times when the future seems thick as a fog; you sit and wait, hoping the mists will lift and reveal the right path. But this is a time when the future seems a door you can walk right through into a room called tomorrow.

Great nations of the world are moving toward democracy through the door to freedom. Men and women of the world move toward free markets through the door to prosperity. The people of the world agitate for free expression and free thought through the door to the moral and intellectual satisfactions that only liberty allows.

We know what works: Freedom works. We know what's right: Freedom is right. We know how to secure a more just and prosperous life for man on Earth: through free markets, free speech, free elections, and the exercise of free will unhampered by the state.

For the first time in this century, for the first time in perhaps all history, man does not have to invent a system by which to live. We don't have to talk late into the night about which form of government is better. We don't have to wrest justice from the kings. We only have to summon it from within ourselves. We must act on what we know. I take as my guide the hope of a saint: In crucial things, unity; in important things, diversity; in all things, generosity.

America today is a proud, free nation, decent and civil, a place we cannot help but love. We know in our hearts, not loudly and proudly but as a simple fact, that this country has meaning beyond what we see, and that our strength is a force for good. But have we changed as a nation even in our time? Are we enthralled with material things, less appreciative of the nobility of work and sacrifice?

My friends, we are not the sum of our possessions. They are not the measure of our lives. In our hearts we know what matters. We cannot hope only to leave our children a bigger car, a bigger bank account. We must hope to give them a sense of what it means to be a loyal friend; a loving parent; a citizen who leaves his home, his neighborhood, and town better than he found it. And what do we want the men and women who work with us to say when we're no longer there? That we were more driven to succeed than anyone around us? Or that we stopped to ask if a sick child had gotten better and stayed a moment there to trade a word of friendship?

No President, no government can teach us to remember what is best in what we are. But if the man you have chosen to lead this government can help make a difference; if he can celebrate the quieter, deeper successes that are made not of gold and silk but of better hearts and finer souls; if he can do these things, then he must.

America is never wholly herself unless she is engaged in high moral principle. We as a people have such a purpose today. It is to make kinder the face of the Nation and gentler the face of the world. My friends, we have work to do. There are the homeless, lost and roaming. There are the children who have nothing, no love and no normalcy. There are those who cannot free themselves of enslavement to whatever addiction -- drugs, welfare, the demoralization that rules the slums. There is crime to be conquered, the rough crime of the streets. There are young women to be helped who are about to become mothers of children they can't care for and might not love. They need our care, our guidance, and our education, though we bless them for choosing life.

The old solution, the old way, was to think that public money alone could end these problems. But we have learned that that is not so. And in any case, our funds are low. We have a deficit to bring down. We have more will than wallet, but will is what we need. We will make the hard choices, looking at what we have and perhaps allocating it differently, making our decisions based on honest need and prudent safety. And then we will do the wisest thing of all. We will turn to the only resource we have that in times of need always grows: the goodness and the courage of the American people.

And I am speaking of a new engagement in the lives of others, a new activism, hands-on and involved, that gets the job done. We must bring in the generations, harnessing the unused talent of the elderly and the unfocused energy of the young. For not only leadership is passed from generation to generation but so is stewardship. And the generation born after the Second World War has come of age.

I have spoken of a Thousand Points of Light, of all the community organizations that are spread like stars throughout the Nation, doing good. We will work hand in hand, encouraging, sometimes leading, sometimes being led, rewarding. We will work on this in the White House, in the Cabinet agencies. I will go to the people and the programs that are the brighter points of light, and I'll ask every member of my government to become involved. The old ideas are new again because they're not old, they are timeless: duty, sacrifice, commitment, and a patriotism that finds its expression in taking part and pitching in.

We need a new engagement, too, between the Executive and the Congress. The challenges before us will be thrashed out with the House and the Senate. And we must bring the Federal budget into balance. And we must ensure that America stands before the world united, strong, at peace, and fiscally sound. But of course things may be difficult. We need to compromise; we've had dissension. We need harmony; we've had a chorus of discordant voices.

For Congress, too, has changed in our time. There has grown a certain divisiveness. We have seen the hard looks and heard the statements in which not each other's ideas are challenged but each other's motives. And our great parties have too often been far apart and untrusting of each other. It's been this way since Vietnam. That war cleaves us still. But, friends, that war began in earnest a quarter of a century ago, and surely the statute of limitation has been reached. This is a fact: The final lesson of Vietnam is that no great nation can long afford to be sundered by a memory. A new breeze is blowing, and the old bipartisanship must be made new again.

To my friends, and, yes, I do mean friends -- in the loyal opposition and, yes, I mean loyal -- I put out my hand. I am putting out my hand to you, Mr. Speaker. I am putting out my hand to you, Mr. Majority Leader. For this is the thing: This is the age of the offered hand. And we can't turn back clocks, and I don't want to. But when our fathers were young, Mr. Speaker, our differences ended at the water's edge. And we don't wish to turn back time, but when our mothers were young, Mr. Majority Leader, the Congress and the Executive were capable of working together to produce a budget on which this nation could live. Let us negotiate soon and hard. But in the end, let us produce. The American people await action. They didn't send us here to bicker. They ask us to rise above the merely partisan. "In crucial things, unity" -- and this, my friends, is crucial.

To the world, too, we offer new engagement and a renewed vow: We will stay strong to protect the peace. The offered hand is a reluctant fist; once made -- strong, and can be used with great effect. There are today Americans who are held against their will in foreign lands and Americans who are unaccounted for. Assistance can be shown here and will be long remembered. Good will begets good will. Good faith can be a spiral that endlessly moves on.

Great nations like great men must keep their word. When America says something, America means it, whether a treaty or an agreement or a vow made on marble steps. We will always try to speak clearly, for candor is a compliment; but subtlety, too, is good and has its place. While keeping our alliances and friendships around the world strong, ever strong, we will continue the new closeness with the Soviet Union, consistent both with our security and with progress.

One might say that our new relationship in part reflects the triumph of hope and strength over experience. But hope is good, and so is strength and vigilance.

Here today are tens of thousands of our citizens who feel the understandable satisfaction of those who have taken part in democracy and seen their hopes fulfilled. But my thoughts have been turning the past few days to those who would be watching at home, to an older fellow who will throw a salute by himself when the flag goes by and the woman who will tell her sons the words of the battle hymns. I don't mean this to be sentimental. I mean that on days like this we remember that we are all part of a continuum, inescapably connected by the ties that bind.

Our children are watching in schools throughout our great land. And to them I say, Thank you for watching democracy's big day. For democracy belongs to us all, and freedom is like a beautiful kite that can go higher and higher with the breeze. And to all I say, No matter what your circumstances or where you are, you are part of this day, you are part of the life of our great nation.

A President is neither prince nor pope, and I don't seek a window on men's souls. In fact, I yearn for a greater tolerance, and easygoingness about each other's attitudes and way of life.

There are few clear areas in which we as a society must rise up united and express our intolerance. The most obvious now is drugs. And when that first cocaine was smuggled in on a ship, it may as well have been a deadly bacteria, so much has it hurt the body, the soul of our country. And there is much to be done and to be said, but take my word for it: This scourge will stop!

And so, there is much to do. And tomorrow the work begins. And I do not mistrust the future. I do not fear what is ahead. For our problems are large, but our heart is larger. Our challenges are great, but our will is greater. And if our flaws are endless, God's love is truly boundless.

Some see leadership as high drama and the sound of trumpets calling, and sometimes it is that. But I see history as a book with many pages, and each day we fill a page with acts of hopefulness and meaning. The new breeze blows, a page turns, the story unfolds. And so, today a chapter begins, a small and stately story of unity, diversity, and generosity -- shared, and written, together.

Thank you. God bless you. And God bless the United States of America.

President George H. W. Bush, Inaugural Address, 20 January 1989

President Bush mentions the financial condition of our nation a couple of times in the course of this speech. The one of these I feel to be the most insightful, profound, and on target is the following:

"And we must bring the Federal budget into balance.
And we must ensure that America stands before the world
united, strong, at peace, and fiscally sound."

Lets take a look at the results of this administration as it relates to performance against the debt, just as we have done all of the others.

Fiscal Year	Total Debt	Change	% Change
1989	$2,857,430,960,187.32		
1990	$3,233,313,451,777.25	$375,882,491,589.93	13.15%
1991	$3,665,303,351,697.03	$431,989,899,919.78	13.36%
1992	$4,064,620,655,521.66	$399,317,303,824.63	10.89%
1993	$4,411,488,883,139.38	$346,868,227,617.72	8.53%
Total		$1,554,057,922,952.06	54.39%

Well, sadly, just as we have seen in the recent past, the rhetoric doesn't come close to matching the results. We have added another 54% to the national debt.

Years of Existence	Total Debt	Total Change	Per Year Average Increase
1	$75,463,476.52		
200	$2,857,430,960,187.32	$2,857,355,496,710.80	$14,287,154,800.94
204	$4,411,488,883,139.38	$1,554,057,922,952.06	$21,624,945,505.59
	Percentage Change In	The per year Average	51.36%

Depressed yet? It took us 192 years, through the end of President Carter's administration, to accumulate nearly 1 trillion dollars in debt. We actually didn't cross the trillion dollar mark until President Reagan's 1st term. Since then in 3 terms or 12 years, we have well surpassed the 4 trillion dollar mark. You know all of those ridiculous comparisons about something relatively small being laid end to end would reach to the moon and the like? Well I hate those, so I'm not gonna include one here. Although if you want some laughs just google the following, "stacking one trillion dollars". By the way I couldn't find anything for 4 trillion.

Now for the tally through 51 presidential terms and 41 Presidents.

Administration	Increased Debt	Decreased Debt	Party Totals
Democrat	13	6	19
Republican	13	7	20
Other	6	6	12
Total	32	19	51

Well, now that we understand what option B was, lets move on.

Charles F. Stamper

8 - WILLIAM J. CLINTON 1993 – 2001 (PRESIDENT 42 & CONGRESSES 103 THROUGH 106)

"Just the fax ma'am, just the fax!"

John McClain

Die Hard 2

President William J. Clinton, a Democrat and our 42nd President, serving in the 52nd presidential term. This administration began on 20 January 1993 and ran through 20 January 1997. It encompassed the 103rd and 104th Congresses. The 103rd Congress had a Democratic majority in both chambers, while the 104th had a Republican majority in both.

President Clinton's personal failings have been well chronicled and we are not going to go into them here. I think it fair to say that he is a fairly polarizing figure when the question of where he should rank when considering a listing of our more effective Presidents. Once again, with the help of our very narrow focus, we are going to attempt to place an objective measure for consideration on a very subjective list.

William J. Clinton, Inaugural Address, 20 January 1993

My fellow citizens, today we celebrate the mystery of American renewal. This ceremony is held in the depth of winter, but by the words we speak and the faces we show the world, we force the spring, a spring reborn in the world's oldest democracy that brings forth the vision and courage to reinvent America. When our Founders boldly declared America's independence to the world and our purposes to the Almighty, they knew that America, to endure, would have to change; not change for change's sake but change to preserve America's ideals: life, liberty, the pursuit of happiness. Though we marched to the music of our time, our mission is timeless. Each generation of Americans must define what it means to be an American.

On behalf of our Nation, I salute my predecessor, President Bush, for his half-century of service to America. And I thank the millions of men and women whose steadfastness and sacrifice triumphed over depression, fascism, and communism.

Today, a generation raised in the shadows of the cold war assumes new responsibilities in a world warmed by the sunshine of freedom but threatened still by ancient hatreds and new plagues. Raised in unrivaled prosperity, we inherit an economy that is still the world's strongest but is weakened by business failures, stagnant wages, increasing inequality, and deep divisions among our own people.

When George Washington first took the oath I have just sworn to uphold, news traveled slowly across the land by horseback and across the ocean by boat. Now, the sights and sounds of this ceremony are broadcast instantaneously to billions around the world. Communications and commerce are global. Investment is mobile. Technology is almost magical. And ambition for a better life is now universal.

We earn our livelihood in America today in peaceful competition with people all across the Earth. Profound and powerful forces are shaking and remaking our world. And the urgent question of our time is whether we can make change our friend and not our enemy. This new world has already enriched the lives of millions of Americans who are able to compete and win in it. But when most people are working harder for less; when others cannot work at all; when the cost of health care devastates families and threatens to bankrupt our enterprises, great and small; when the fear of crime robs law-abiding citizens of their freedom; and when millions of poor children cannot even imagine the lives we are calling them to lead, we have not made change our friend.

We know we have to face hard truths and take strong steps, but we have not done so; instead, we have drifted. And that drifting has eroded our resources, fractured our economy, and shaken our confidence. Though our challenges are fearsome, so are our strengths. Americans have ever been a restless, questing, hopeful people. And we must bring to our task today the vision and will of those who came before us. From our Revolution to the Civil War, to the Great Depression, to the civil rights movement, our people have always mustered the determination to construct from these crises the pillars of our history. Thomas Jefferson believed that to preserve the very foundations of our Nation, we would need dramatic change from time to time. Well, my fellow Americans, this is our time. Let us embrace it.

Our democracy must be not only the envy of the world but the engine of our own renewal. There is nothing wrong with America that cannot be cured by what is right with America. And so today we pledge an end to the era of deadlock and drift, and a new season of American renewal has begun.

To renew America, we must be bold. We must do what no generation has had to do before. We must invest more in our own people, in their jobs, and in their future, and at the same time cut our massive debt. And we must do so in a world in which we must compete for every opportunity. It will not be easy. It will require sacrifice, but it can be done and done fairly, not choosing sacrifice for its own sake but for our own sake. We must provide for our Nation the way a family provides for its children.

Our Founders saw themselves in the light of posterity. We can do no less. Anyone who has ever watched a child's eyes wander into sleep knows what posterity is. Posterity is the world to come: the world for whom we hold our ideals, from whom we have borrowed our planet, and to whom we bear sacred responsibility. We must do what America does best: offer more opportunity to all and demand more responsibility from all. It is time to break the bad habit of expecting something for nothing from our Government or from each other. Let us all take more responsibility not only for ourselves and our families but for our communities and our country.

To renew America, we must revitalize our democracy. This beautiful Capital, like every capital since the dawn of civilization, is often a place of intrigue and calculation. Powerful people maneuver for position and worry endlessly about who is in and who is out, who is up and who is down, forgetting those people whose toil and sweat sends us here and pays our way. Americans deserve better. And in this city today there are people who want to do better. And so I say to all of you here: Let us resolve to reform our politics so that power and privilege no longer shout down the voice of the people. Let us put aside personal advantage so that we can feel the pain and see the promise of America. Let us resolve to make our Government a place for what Franklin Roosevelt called bold, persistent experimentation, a Government for our tomorrows, not our yesterdays. Let us give this Capital back to the people to whom it belongs.

To renew America, we must meet challenges abroad as well as at home. There is no longer a clear division between what is foreign and what is domestic. The world economy, the world environment, the world AIDS crisis, the world arms race: they affect us all. Today, as an older order passes, the new world is more free but less stable. Communism's collapse has called forth old animosities and new dangers. Clearly, America must continue to lead the world we did so much to make.

While America rebuilds at home, we will not shrink from the challenges nor fail to seize the opportunities of this new world. Together with our friends and allies, we will work to shape change, lest it engulf us. When our vital interests are challenged or the will and conscience of the international community is defied, we will act, with peaceful diplomacy whenever possible, with force when necessary. The brave Americans serving our Nation today in the Persian Gulf, in Somalia, and wherever else they stand are testament to our resolve. But our greatest strength is the power of our ideas, which are still new in many lands. Across the world we see them embraced, and we rejoice. Our hopes, our hearts, our hands are with those on every continent who are building democracy and freedom. Their cause is America's cause.

The American people have summoned the change we celebrate today. You have raised your voices in an unmistakable chorus. You have cast your votes in historic numbers. And you have changed the face of Congress, the Presidency, and the political process itself. Yes, you, my fellow Americans, have forced the spring. Now we must do the work the season demands. To that work I now turn with all the authority of my office. I ask the Congress to join with me. But no President, no Congress, no Government can undertake this mission alone.

My fellow Americans, you, too, must play your part in our renewal. I challenge a new generation of young Americans to a season of service: to act on your idealism by helping troubled children, keeping company with those in need, reconnecting our torn communities. There is so much to be done; enough, indeed, for millions of others who are still young in spirit to give of themselves in service, too. In serving, we recognize a simple but powerful truth: We need each other, and we must care for one another.

Today we do more than celebrate America. We rededicate ourselves to the very idea of America, an idea born in revolution and renewed through two centuries of challenge; an idea tempered by the knowledge that, but for fate, we, the fortunate, and the unfortunate might have been each other; an idea ennobled by the faith that our Nation can summon from its myriad diversity the deepest measure of unity; an idea infused with the conviction that America's long, heroic journey must go forever upward.

And so, my fellow Americans, as we stand at the edge of the 21st century, let us begin anew with energy and hope, with faith and discipline. And let us work until our work is done. The Scripture says, "And let us not be weary in well doing: for in due season we shall reap, if we faint not." From this joyful mountaintop of celebration we hear a call to service in the valley. We have heard the trumpets. We have changed the guard. And now, each in our own way and with God's help, we must answer the call.

Thank you, and God bless you all.

William J. Clinton, Inaugural Address, 20 January 1993

The following snippet from this speech indicates that President Clinton held the nations debt situation in the front of mind:

> *"To renew America, we must be bold. We must do what no generation has had to do before. We must invest more in our own people, in their jobs, and in their future, and at the same time cut our massive debt. "*

President Clinton is the first Democrat to hold the office of President since the administration of President Carter, another governor of a southern state, which is largely viewed by most as a failed administration. One that was not successful in balancing a budget and significantly added to the national debt. Let's see how this administration performed.

Fiscal Year	Total Debt	Change	% Change
1993	$4,411,488,883,139.38		
1994	$4,692,749,910,013.32	$281,261,026,873.94	6.38%
1995	$4,973,982,900,709.39	$281,232,990,696.07	5.99%
1996	$5,224,810,939,135.73	$250,828,038,426.34	5.04%
1997	$5,413,146,011,397.34	$188,335,072,261.61	3.60%
Total		$1,001,657,128,257.96	22.71%

As you can see from the table above this administration saw the continued upward rise of the national debt. Although the percentage of change is significantly lower than the previous 4 administrations which I have defined as the "modern Presidents". By way of review, President Carter up by 42%, Reagan up by 82% and 56% for the 1st and second terms alone with an increase of 186% for the 8 year term as a whole, President H. W. Bush at 54%, followed by this first Clinton term at 23%. A significant slowing of the rate of growth of the debt but still added slightly over 1 trillion dollars to it.

Years of Existence	Total Debt	Total Change	Per Year Average Increase
1	$75,463,476.52		
204	$4,411,488,883,139.38	$4,411,413,419,662.86	$21,624,945,505.59
208	$5,413,146,011,397.34	$1,001,657,128,257.96	$26,024,740,439.41
	Percentage Change In	The per year Average	20.35%

Now for the tally through 52 presidential terms and 42 Presidents.

Administration	Increased Debt	Decreased Debt	Party Totals
Democrat	14	6	20
Republican	13	7	20
Other	6	6	12
Total	33	19	52

A Dime's Difference?

President William J. Clinton, a Democrat and our 42nd President, serving in the 53rd presidential term. This administration began on 20 January 1997 and ran through 20 January 2001 It encompassed the 105th and 106th Congresses. Both houses of both these Congresses held Republican majorities.

Let's take a look at President Clinton's 2nd inaugural address.

William J. Clinton, Inaugural Address, 20 January 1997

My fellow citizens, at this last Presidential Inauguration of the 20th century, let us lift our eyes toward the challenges that await us in the next century. It is our great good fortune that time and chance have put us not only at the edge of a new century, in a new millennium, but on the edge of a bright new prospect in human affairs, a moment that will define our course and our character for decades to comes. We must keep our old democracy forever young. Guided by the ancient vision of a promised land, let us set our sights upon a land of new promise.

The promise of America was born in the 18th century out of the bold conviction that we are all created equal. It was extended and preserved in the 19th century, when our Nation spread across the continent, saved the Union, and abolished the awful scourge of slavery.

Then, in turmoil and triumph, that promise exploded onto the world stage to make this the American Century. And what a century it has been. America became the world's mightiest industrial power, saved the world from tyranny in two World Wars and a long cold war, and time and again reached out across the globe to millions who, like us, longed for the blessings of liberty.

Along the way, Americans produced a great middle class and security in old age, built unrivaled centers of learning and opened public schools to all, split the atom and explored the heavens, invented the computer and the microchip, and deepened the wellspring of justice by making a revolution in civil rights for African-Americans and all minorities and extending the circle of citizenship, opportunity, and dignity to women.

Now, for the third time, a new century is upon us and another time to choose. We began the 19th century with a choice: to spread our Nation from coast to coast. We began the 20th century with a choice: to harness the industrial revolution to our values of free enterprise, conservation, and human decency. Those choices made all the difference. At the dawn of the 21st century, a free people must now choose to shape the forces of the information age and the global society, to unleash the limitless potential of all our people, and yes, to form a more perfect Union.

When last we gathered, our march to this new future seemed less certain than it does today. We vowed then to set a clear course to renew our Nation. In these 4 years, we have been touched by tragedy, exhilarated by challenge, strengthened by achievement. America stands alone as the world's indispensable nation. Once again, our economy is the strongest on Earth. Once again, we are building stronger families, thriving communities, better educational opportunities, a cleaner environment. Problems that once seemed destined to deepen, now bend to our efforts. Our streets are safer, and record numbers of our fellow citizens have moved from welfare to work. And once again, we have resolved for our time a great debate over the role of Government. Today we can declare: Government is not the problem, and Government is not the solution. We—the American people—we are the solution. Our Founders understood that well and gave us a democracy strong enough to endure for centuries, flexible enough to face our common challenges and advance our common dreams in each new day.

As times change, so Government must change. We need a new Government for a new century, humble enough not to try to solve all our problems for us but strong enough to give us the tools to solve our problems for ourselves, a Government that is smaller, lives within its means, and does more with less. Yet where it can stand up for our values and interests around the world, and where it can give Americans the power to make a real difference in their everyday lives,

Government should do more, not less. The preeminent mission of our new Government is to give all Americans an opportunity, not a guarantee but a real opportunity, to build better lives.

Beyond that, my fellow citizens, the future is up to us. Our Founders taught us that the preservation of our liberty and our Union depends upon responsible citizenship. And we need a new sense of responsibility for a new century. There is work to do, work that Government alone cannot do: teaching children to read, hiring people off welfare rolls, coming out from behind locked doors and shuttered windows to help reclaim our streets from drugs and gangs and crime, taking time out of our own lives to serve others.

Each and every one of us, in our own way, must assume personal responsibility not only for ourselves and our families but for our neighbors and our Nation. Our greatest responsibility is to embrace a new spirit of community for a new century. For any one of us to succeed, we must succeed as one America. The challenge of our past remains the challenge of our future: Will we be one Nation, one people, with one common destiny, or not? Will we all come together, or come apart?

The divide of race has been America's constant curse. And each new wave of immigrants gives new targets to old prejudices. Prejudice and contempt cloaked in the pretense of religious or political conviction are no different. These forces have nearly destroyed our Nation in the past. They plague us still. They fuel the fanaticism of terror. And they torment the lives of millions in fractured nations all around the world.

These obsessions cripple both those who hate and of course those who are hated, robbing both of what they might become. We cannot, we will not, succumb to the dark impulses that lurk in the far regions of the soul everywhere. We shall overcome them. And we shall replace them with the generous spirit of a people who feel at home with one another. Our rich texture of racial, religious, and political diversity will be a godsend in the 21st century. Great rewards will come to those who can live together, learn together, work together, forge new ties that bind together.

As this new era approaches, we can already see its broad outlines. Ten years ago, the Internet was the mystical province of physicists; today, it is a commonplace encyclopedia for millions of schoolchildren. Scientists now are decoding the blueprint of human life. Cures for our most feared illnesses seem close at hand. The world is no longer divided into two hostile camps. Instead, now we are building bonds with nations that once were our adversaries. Growing connections of commerce and culture give us a chance to lift the fortunes and spirits of people the world over. And for the very first time in all of history, more people on this planet live under democracy than dictatorship.

My fellow Americans, as we look back at this remarkable century, we may ask, can we hope not just to follow but even to surpass the achievements of the 20th century in America and to avoid the awful bloodshed that stained its legacy? To that question, every American here and every American in our land today must answer a resounding, "Yes!" This is the heart of our task. With a new vision of Government, a new sense of responsibility, a new spirit of community, we will sustain America's journey.

The promise we sought in a new land, we will find again in a land of new promise. In this new land, education will be every citizen's most prized possession. Our schools will have the highest standards in the world, igniting the spark of possibility in the eyes of every girl and every boy. And the doors of higher education will be open to all. The knowledge and power of the information age will be within reach not just of the few but of every classroom, every library, every child. Parents and children will have time not only to work but to read and play together. And the plans they make at their kitchen table will be those of a better home, a better job, the certain chance to go to college.

Our streets will echo again with the laughter of our children, because no one will try to shoot them or sell them drugs anymore. Everyone who can work, will work, with today's permanent under class part of tomorrow's growing middle class. New miracles of medicine at last will reach not only those who can claim care now but the children and hard-working families too long denied.

We will stand mighty for peace and freedom and maintain a strong defense against terror and destruction. Our children will sleep free from the threat of nuclear, chemical, or biological weapons. Ports and airports, farms and factories will thrive with trade and innovation and ideas. And the world's greatest democracy will lead a whole world of democracies.

Our land of new promise will be a nation that meets its obligations, a nation that balances its budget but never loses the balance of its values, a nation where our grandparents have secure retirement and health care and their grandchildren know we have made the reforms necessary to sustain those benefits for their time, a nation that fortifies the world's most productive economy even as it protects the great natural bounty of our water, air, and majestic land. And in this land of new promise, we will have reformed our politics so that the voice of the people will always speak louder than the din of narrow interests, regaining the participation and deserving the trust of all Americans.

Fellow citizens, let us build that America, a nation ever moving forward toward realizing the full potential of all its citizens. Prosperity and power, yes, they are important, and we must maintain them. But let us never forget, the greatest progress we have made and the greatest progress we have yet to make is in the human heart. In the end, all the world's wealth and a thousand armies are no match for the strength and decency of the human spirit.

Thirty-four years ago, the man whose life we celebrate today spoke to us down there, at the other end of this Mall, in words that moved the conscience of a nation. Like a prophet of old, he told of his dream that one day America would rise up and treat all its citizens as equals before the law and in the heart. Martin Luther King's dream was the American dream. His quest is our quest: the ceaseless striving to live out our true creed. Our history has been built on such dreams and labors. And by our dreams and labors, we will redeem the promise of America in the 21st century.

To that effort I pledge all my strength and every power of my office. I ask the Members of Congress here to join in that pledge. The American people returned to office a President of one party and a Congress of another. Surely they did not do this to advance the politics of petty bickering and extreme partisanship they plainly deplore. No, they call on us instead to be repairers of the breach and to move on with America's mission. America demands and deserves big things from us, and nothing big ever came from being small. Let us remember the timeless wisdom of Cardinal Bernardin, when facing the end of his own life. He said, "It is wrong to waste the precious gift of time on acrimony and division."

Fellow citizens, we must not waste the precious gift of this time. For all of us are on that same journey of our lives, and our journey, too, will come to an end. But the journey of our America must go on.

And so, my fellow Americans, we must be strong, for there is much to dare. The demands of our time are great, and they are different. Let us meet them with faith and courage, with patience and a grateful, happy heart. Let us shape the hope of this day into the noblest chapter in our history. Yes, let us build our bridge, a bridge wide enough and strong enough for every American to cross over to a blessed land of new promise.

May those generations whose faces we cannot yet see, whose names we may never know, say of us here that we led our beloved land into a new century with the American dream alive for all her children, with the American promise of a more perfect Union a reality for all her people, with America's bright flame of freedom spreading throughout all the world.

From the height of this place and the summit of this century, let us go forth. May God strengthen our hands for the good work ahead, and always, always bless our America.

William J. Clinton, Inaugural Address, 20 January 1997

From this speech President Clinton again speaks of a balanced budget:

*"Our land of new promise will be a nation that meets its obligations,
a nation that balances its budget but never loses the balance of its values,"*

Let's take a look at the results, shall we.

Fiscal Year	Total Debt	Change	% Change
1997	$5,413,146,011,397.34		
1998	$5,526,193,008,897.62	$113,046,997,500.28	2.09%
1999	$5,656,270,901,615.43	$130,077,892,717.81	2.35%
2000	$5,674,178,209,886.86	$17,907,308,271.43	0.32%
2001	$5,807,463,412,200.06	$133,285,202,313.20	2.35%
Total		$394,317,400,802.72	7.28%

Not bad at all, 7% in total, with one year being 0.32%, but still continuing the upward trajectory of the debt. Now you have probably heard that in 2000 there was a budget surplus, well in federal government speak there was. So then why did the debt rise in 2000 you ask? If you remember quite early in this book I mentioned that some things the federal government spends money on is so called "off budget". Well there ya go.

As for our per year average:

Years of Existence	Total Debt	Total Change	Per Year Average Increase
1	$75,463,476.52		
208	$5,413,146,011,397.34	$5,413,070,547,920.82	$26,024,740,439.41
212	$5,807,463,412,200.06	$394,317,400,802.72	$27,393,695,340.57
	Percentage Change In	The per year Average	5.26%

Now lets take a look at both terms by President Clinton taken as a single unit, in a like fashion to our review of President Reagan. By the way, we will be doing the same for President George W. Bush.

When President Clinton to office in 1993 the national debt stood at $4,411,488,883,139.38. When he left office 8 years later in 2001 the debt stood at $5,807,463,412,200.06. This is an increase of $1,395,974,529,060.68, for a percentage change of 31.6% over the entire 8 year period.

Now for the tally through 53 presidential terms and 42 Presidents.

Administration	Increased Debt	Decreased Debt	Party Totals
Democrat	15	6	21
Republican	13	7	20
Other	6	6	12
Total	34	19	53

These are the facts and only the facts. Regardless of what the definition of is is.

9 – GEORGE W. BUSH 2001 – 2009 (PRESIDENT 43 & CONGRESSES 107 THROUGH 110)

"None of this ever happened, gentlemen. And I don't want to see any paperwork on it. "

Roz

Monsters Inc.

President George W. Bush, a Republican and our 43rd President, serving in the 54th presidential term. This administration began on 20 January 2001 and ran through 20 January 2005 It encompassed the 107th and 108th Congresses. The 107th Congress featured a very rare even split in the Senate between the 2 parties and as a result the majority changed hands on 3 occasions, the House was Republican. The 108th had Republican majorities in both houses.

As is our tradition with the "modern" Presidents we will begin by reading the first inaugural address from President George W. Bush.

President G. W. Bush, inaugural address, 20 January 2001

Thank you, all. Chief Justice Rehnquist, President Carter, President Bush, President Clinton, distinguished guests, and my fellow citizens. The peaceful transfer of authority is rare in history, yet common in our country. With a simple oath, we affirm old traditions and make new beginnings.

As I begin, I thank President Clinton for his service to our Nation, and I thank Vice President Gore for a contest conducted with spirit and ended with grace.

I am honored and humbled to stand here where so many of America's leaders have come before me, and so many will follow. We have a place, all of us, in a long story, a story we continue but whose end we will not see. It is a story of a new world that became a friend and liberator of the old, the story of a slave holding society that became a servant of freedom, the story of a power that went into the world to protect but not possess, to defend but not to conquer.

It is the American story, a story of flawed and fallible people united across the generations by grand and enduring ideals. The grandest of these ideals is an unfolding American promise that everyone belongs, that everyone deserves a chance, that no insignificant person was ever born.

Americans are called to enact this promise in our lives and in our laws. And though our Nation has sometimes halted and sometimes delayed, we must follow no other course.

Through much of the last century, America's faith in freedom and democracy was a rock in a raging sea. Now it is a seed upon the wind, taking root in many nations. Our democratic faith is more than the creed of our country. It is the inborn hope of our humanity, an ideal we carry but do not own, a trust we bear and pass along. Even after nearly 225 years, we have a long way yet to travel.

While many of our citizens prosper, others doubt the promise, even the justice of our own country. The ambitions of some Americans are limited by failing schools and hidden prejudice and the circumstances of their birth. And sometimes our differences run so deep, it seems we share a continent but not a country. We do not accept this, and we will not allow it.

Our unity, our Union, is a serious work of leaders and citizens and every generation. And this is my solemn pledge: I will work to build a single nation of justice and opportunity. I know this is in our reach because we are guided by a power larger than ourselves, who creates us equal, in His image, and we are confident in principles that unite and lead us onward.

America has never been united by blood or birth or soil. We are bound by ideals that move us beyond our backgrounds, lift us above our interests, and teach us what it means to be citizens. Every child must be taught these principles. Every citizen must uphold them. And every immigrant, by embracing these ideals, makes our country more, not less, American.

Today we affirm a new commitment to live out our Nation's promise through civility, courage, compassion, and character. America at its best matches a commitment to principle with a concern for civility. A civil society demands from each of us good will and respect, fair dealing and forgiveness.

Some seem to believe that our politics can afford to be petty because in a time of peace the stakes of our debates appear small. But the stakes for America are never small. If our country does not lead the cause of freedom, it will not be led. If we do not turn the hearts of children toward knowledge and character, we will lose their gifts and undermine their idealism. If we permit our economy to drift and decline, the vulnerable will suffer most.

We must live up to the calling we share. Civility is not a tactic or a sentiment; it is the determined choice of trust over cynicism, of community over chaos. And this commitment, if we keep it, is a way to shared accomplishment.

America at its best is also courageous. Our national courage has been clear in times of depression and war, when defeating common dangers defined our common good. Now we must choose if the example of our fathers and mothers will inspire us or condemn us. We must show courage in a time of blessing by confronting problems instead of passing them on to future generations.

Together we will reclaim America's schools before ignorance and apathy claim more young lives. We will reform Social Security and Medicare, sparing our children from struggles we have the power to prevent. And we will reduce taxes to recover the momentum of our economy and reward the effort and enterprise of working Americans.

We will build our defenses beyond challenge, lest weakness invite challenge. We will confront weapons of mass destruction, so that a new century is spared new horrors. The enemies of liberty and our country should make no mistake: America remains engaged in the world, by history and by choice, shaping a balance of power that favors freedom.

We will defend our allies and our interests. We will show purpose without arrogance. We will meet aggression and bad faith with resolve and strength. And to all nations, we will speak for the values that gave our Nation birth.

America at its best is compassionate. In the quiet of American conscience, we know that deep, persistent poverty is unworthy of our Nation's promise. And whatever our views of its cause, we can agree that children at risk are not at fault.

Abandonment and abuse are not acts of God; they are failures of love. And the proliferation of prisons, however necessary, is no substitute for hope and order in our souls. Where there is suffering, there is duty. Americans in need are not strangers; they are citizens— not problems but priorities. And all of us are diminished when any are hopeless.

Government has great responsibilities for public safety and public health, for civil rights and common schools. Yet, compassion is the work of a nation, not just a government. And some needs and hurts are so deep they will only respond to a mentor's touch or a pastor's prayer. Church and charity, synagogue and mosque lend our communities their humanity, and they will have an honored place in our plans and in our laws.

Many in our country do not know the pain of poverty. But we can listen to those who do. And I can pledge our Nation to a goal: When we see that wounded traveler on the road to Jericho, we will not pass to the other side.

America at its best is a place where personal responsibility is valued and expected. Encouraging responsibility is not a search for scapegoats; it is a call to conscience. And though it requires sacrifice, it brings a deeper fulfillment. We find the fullness of life not only in options but in commitments. And we find that children and community are the commitments that set us free.

Our public interest depends on private character, on civic duty and family bonds and basic fairness, on uncounted, unhonored acts of decency, which give direction to our freedom.

Sometimes in life we're called to do great things. But as a saint of our times has said, "Every day we are called to do small things with great love." The most important tasks of a democracy are done by everyone.

I will live and lead by these principles: to advance my convictions with civility, to serve the public interest with courage, to speak for greater justice and compassion, to call for responsibility and try to live it, as well. In all these ways, I will bring the values of our history to the care of our times.

What you do is as important as anything Government does. I ask you to seek a common good beyond your comfort, to defend needed reforms against easy attacks, to serve your Nation, beginning with your neighbor. I ask you to be citizens: Citizens, not spectators; citizens, not subjects; responsible citizens building communities of service and a nation of character.

Americans are generous and strong and decent, not because we believe in ourselves but because we hold beliefs beyond ourselves. When this spirit of citizenship is missing, no Government program can replace it. When this spirit is present, no wrong can stand against it.

After the Declaration of Independence was signed, Virginia statesman John Page wrote to Thomas Jefferson, "We know the race is not to the swift, nor the battle to the strong. Do you not think an angel rides in the whirlwind and directs this storm?"

Much time has passed since Jefferson arrived for his inauguration. The years and changes accumulate, but the themes of this day, he would know: our Nation's grand story of courage and its simple dream of dignity.

We are not this story's author, who fills time and eternity with his purpose. Yet, his purpose is achieved in our duty. And our duty is fulfilled in service to one another. Never tiring, never yielding, never finishing, we renew that purpose today, to make our country more just and generous, to affirm the dignity of our lives and every life. This work continues, the story goes on, and an angel still rides in the whirlwind and directs this storm.

God bless you all, and God bless America.

President G. W. Bush, inaugural address, 20 January 2001

Well, President George W. Bush didn't reference the national debt by name but did mention it in passing. Let's see how this administration performed.

Fiscal Year	Total Debt	Change	% Change
2001	$5,807,463,412,200.06		
2002	$6,228,235,965,597.16	$420,772,553,397.10	7.25%
2003	$6,783,231,062,743.62	$554,995,097,146.46	8.91%
2004	$7,379,052,696,330.32	$595,821,633,586.70	8.78%
2005	$7,932,709,661,723.50	$553,656,965,393.18	7.50%
Total		$2,125,246,249,523.44	36.60%

Still going in the wrong direction and we have stepped on the accelerator once again with the national debt increasing by over 36%.

As for or per year average:

Years of Existence	Total Debt	Total Change	Per Year Average Increase
1	$75,463,476.52		
212	$5,807,463,412,200.06	$5,807,387,948,723.54	$27,393,695,340.57
216	$7,932,709,661,723.50	$2,125,246,249,523.44	$36,725,507,693.16
	Percentage Change In	The per year Average	34.07%

Now for the tally through 54 presidential terms and 43 Presidents.

Administration	Increased Debt	Decreased Debt	Party Totals
Democrat	15	6	21
Republican	14	7	21
Other	6	6	12
Total	35	19	54

President George W. Bush, a Republican and our 43rd President, serving in the 55th presidential term. This administration began on 20 January 2005 and ran through 20 January 2009 It encompassed the 109th and 110th Congresses. The 109th Congress had Republican majorities in both houses while the 110th had Democratic majorities in both.

President George W. Bush, Inaugural Address, 20 January 2005

Vice President Cheney, Mr. Chief Justice, President Carter, President Bush, President Clinton, Members of the United States Congress, reverend clergy, distinguished guests, fellow citizens:

On this day, prescribed by law and marked by ceremony, we celebrate the durable wisdom of our Constitution and recall the deep commitments that unite our country. I am grateful for the honor of this hour, mindful of the consequential times in which we live, and determined to fulfill the oath that I have sworn and you have witnessed.

At this second gathering, our duties are defined not by the words I use but by the history we have seen together. For a half a century, America defended our own freedom by standing watch on distant borders. After the shipwreck of communism came years of relative quiet, years of repose, years of sabbatical, and then there came a day of fire.

We have seen our vulnerability, and we have seen its deepest source. For as long as whole regions of the world simmer in resentment and tyranny, prone to ideologies that feed hatred and excuse murder, violence will gather and multiply in destructive power and cross the most defended borders and raise a mortal threat. There is only one force of history that can break the reign of hatred and resentment and expose the pretensions of tyrants and reward the hopes of the decent and tolerant, and that is the force of human freedom.

We are led, by events and common sense, to one conclusion: The survival of liberty in our land increasingly depends on the success of liberty in other lands. The best hope for peace in our world is the expansion of freedom in all the world.

America's vital interests and our deepest beliefs are now one. From the day of our founding, we have proclaimed that every man and woman on this Earth has rights and dignity and matchless value, because they bear the image of the Maker of heaven and Earth. Across the generations, we have proclaimed the imperative of self-government, because no one is fit to be a master and no one deserves to be a slave. Advancing these ideals is the mission that created our Nation. It is the honorable achievement of our fathers. Now, it is the urgent requirement of our Nation's security and the calling of our time.

So it is the policy of the United States to seek and support the growth of democratic movements and institutions in every nation and culture, with the ultimate goal of ending tyranny in our world. This is not primarily the task of arms, though we will defend ourselves and our friends by force of arms when necessary. Freedom, by its nature, must be chosen and defended by citizens and sustained by the rule of law and the protection of minorities. And when the soul of a nation finally speaks, the institutions that arise may reflect customs and traditions very different from our own. America will not impose our own style of government on the unwilling. Our goal instead is to help others find their own voice, attain their own freedom, and make their own way.

The great objective of ending tyranny is the concentrated work of generations. The difficulty of the task is no excuse for avoiding it. America's influence is not unlimited, but fortunately for the oppressed, America's influence is considerable and we will use it confidently in freedom's cause.

My most solemn duty is to protect this Nation and its people from further attacks and emerging threats. Some have unwisely chosen to test America's resolve and have found it firm. We will persistently clarify the choice before every ruler and every nation, the moral choice between oppression, which is always wrong, and freedom, which is eternally right.

America will not pretend that jailed dissidents prefer their chains or that women welcome humiliation and servitude or that any human being aspires to live at the mercy of bullies. We will encourage reform in other governments by making clear that success in our relations will require the decent treatment of their own people. America's belief in human dignity will guide our policies. Yet rights must be more than the grudging concessions of dictators. They are secured by free dissent and the participation of the governed. In the long run, there is no justice without freedom and there can be no human rights without human liberty.

Some, I know, have questioned the global appeal of liberty, though this time in history, four decades defined by the swiftest advance of freedom ever seen, is an odd time for doubt. Americans, of all people, should never be surprised by the power of our ideals. Eventually, the call of freedom comes to every mind and every soul. We do not accept the existence of permanent tyranny because we do not accept the possibility of permanent slavery. Liberty will come to those who love it.

Today, America speaks anew to the peoples of the world. All who live in tyranny and hopelessness can know: The United States will not ignore your oppression or excuse your oppressors. When you stand for your liberty, we will stand with you.

Democratic reformers facing repression, prison, or exile can know: America sees you for who you are, the future leaders of your free country.

The rulers of outlaw regimes can know that we still believe as Abraham Lincoln did: "Those who deny freedom to others deserve it not for themselves and, under the rule of a just God, cannot long retain it."

The leaders of governments with long habits of control need to know: To serve your people, you must learn to trust them. Start on this journey of progress and justice, and America will walk at your side.

And all the allies of the United States can know: We honor your friendship; we rely on your counsel; and we depend on your help. Division among free nations is a primary goal of freedom's enemies. The concerted effort of free nations to promote democracy is a prelude to our enemies' defeat.

Today I also speak anew to my fellow citizens. From all of you I have asked patience in the hard task of securing America, which you have granted in good measure. Our country has accepted obligations that are difficult to fulfill and would be dishonorable to abandon. Yet because we have acted in the great liberating tradition of this Nation, tens of millions have achieved their freedom. And as hope kindles hope, millions more will find it. By our efforts, we have lit a fire as well, a fire in the minds of men. It warms those who feel its power. It burns those who fight its progress. And one day this untamed fire of freedom will reach the darkest corners of our world.

A few Americans have accepted the hardest duties in this cause, in the quiet work of intelligence and diplomacy, the idealistic work of helping raise up free governments, the dangerous and necessary work of fighting our enemies. Some have shown their devotion to our country in deaths that honored their whole lives, and we will always honor their names and their sacrifice.

All Americans have witnessed this idealism and some for the first time. I ask our youngest citizens to believe the evidence of your eyes. You have seen duty and allegiance in the determined faces of our soldiers. You have seen that life is fragile and evil is real and courage triumphs. Make the choice to serve in a cause larger than your wants, larger than yourself, and in your days you will add not just to the wealth of our country but to its character.

America has need of idealism and courage because we have essential work at home, the unfinished work of American freedom. In a world moving toward liberty, we are determined to show the meaning and promise of liberty.

In America's ideal of freedom, citizens find the dignity and security of economic independence instead of laboring on the edge of subsistence. This is the broader definition of liberty that motivated the Homestead Act, the Social Security Act, and the GI bill of rights. And now we will extend this vision by reforming great institutions to serve the needs of our time. To give every American a stake in the promise and future of our country, we will bring the highest standards to our schools and build an ownership society. We will widen the ownership of homes and businesses, retirement savings, and health insurance, preparing our people for the challenges of life in a free society. By making every citizen an agent of his or her own destiny, we will give our fellow Americans greater freedom from want and fear and make our society more prosperous and just and equal.

In America's ideal of freedom, the public interest depends on private character, on integrity and tolerance toward others and the rule of conscience in our own lives. Self-government relies, in the end, on the governing of the self. That edifice of character is built in families, supported by communities with standards, and sustained in our national life by the truths of Sinai, the Sermon on the Mount, the words of the Koran, and the varied faiths of our people. Americans move forward in every generation by reaffirming all that is good and true that came before, ideals of justice and conduct that are the same yesterday, today, and forever.

In America's ideal of freedom, the exercise of rights is ennobled by service and mercy and a heart for the weak. Liberty for all does not mean independence from one another. Our Nation relies on men and women who look after a neighbor and surround the lost with love. Americans, at our best, value the life we see in one another and must always remember that even the unwanted have worth. And our country must abandon all the habits of racism, because we cannot carry the message of freedom and the baggage of bigotry at the same time.

From the perspective of a single day, including this day of dedication, the issues and questions before our country are many. From the viewpoint of centuries, the questions that come to us are narrowed and few: Did our generation advance the cause of freedom? And did our character bring credit to that cause?

These questions that judge us also unite us, because Americans of every party and background, Americans by choice and by birth are bound to one another in the cause of freedom. We have known divisions, which must be healed to move forward in great purposes, and I will strive in good faith to heal them. Yet those divisions do not define America. We felt the unity and fellowship of our Nation when freedom came under attack, and our response came like a single hand over a single heart. And we can feel that same unity and pride whenever America acts for good and the victims of disaster are given hope and the unjust encounter justice and the captives are set free.

We go forward with complete confidence in the eventual triumph of freedom, not because history runs on the wheels of inevitability—it is human choices that move events; not because we consider ourselves a chosen nation—God moves and chooses as He wills. We have confidence because freedom is the permanent hope of mankind, the hunger in dark places, the longing of the soul. When our Founders declared a new order of the ages, when soldiers died in wave upon wave for a union based on liberty, when citizens marched in peaceful outrage under the banner "Freedom Now," they were acting on an ancient hope that is meant to be fulfilled. History has an ebb and flow of justice, but history also has a visible direction, set by liberty and the Author of Liberty.

When the Declaration of Independence was first read in public and the Liberty Bell was sounded in celebration, a witness said, "It rang as if it meant something." In our time, it means something still. America, in this young century, proclaims liberty throughout all the world and to all the inhabitants thereof. Renewed in our strength, tested but not weary, we are ready for the greatest achievements in the history of freedom. May God bless you, and may He watch over the United States of America.

President George W. Bush, Inaugural Address, 20 January 2005

Fiscal Year	Total Debt	Change	% Change
2005	$7,932,709,661,723.50		
2006	$8,506,973,899,215.23	$574,264,237,491.73	7.24%
2007	$9,007,653,372,262.48	$500,679,473,047.25	5.89%
2008	$10,024,724,896,912.40	$1,017,071,524,649.92	11.29%
2009	$11,909,829,003,511.70	$1,885,104,106,599.30	18.80%
Total		$3,977,119,341,788.20	50.14%

Well, there you have it, another administrations piling on to the national debt, increasing it by another 50%.

As for our per year average:

Years of Existence	Total Debt	Total Change	Per Year Average Increase
1	$75,463,476.52		
216	$7,932,709,661,723.50	$7,932,634,198,246.98	$36,725,507,693.16
220	$11,909,829,003,511.70	$3,977,119,341,788.20	$54,135,586,379.60
	Percentage Change In	The per year Average	47.41%

As with the other 2 term Presidents lets take a look at the full 8 year term for President George W. Bush.

When President Bush took office in 2001 the national debt stood at $5,807,463,412,200.06 and here we are 8 years later in 2009 at $11,909,829,003,511.70, for a total change of $6,102,365,591,311.64. That results in a percentage change of 105%. This makes 2, of our last 3, 2 term

Presidents that have more than doubled the national debt in 8 years. First was President Reagan with an increase of over 180% and now President Bush with and increase of 105%. Our 3rd two term administration, led by President Clinton, came in well under both of these 2 with an increase of 31%. Quite large, in and of itself, but very miserly by comparison.

Now for the tally through 55 presidential terms and 43 Presidents.

Administration	Increased Debt	Decreased Debt	Party Totals
Democrat	15	6	21
Republican	15	7	22
Other	6	6	12
Total	36	19	55

Well we are through 43 of our 44 Presidents, 1 more to go. 220 years into our constitutional form of government. With the modern news media, internet, social media, and the like I'm sure you have a pretty well defined pre-conception of this administrations performance against the national debt, but I guess we will go ahead and take a look at it anyway. Who knows there might be a surprise in there somewhere. I doubt it' but I'm trying to stay positive here.

As we prepare to move forward, I'd love to tell you exactly how this fits into those conservative principles I hear so much about these days. Unfortunately I can not, because I don't want to risk running afoul of the "Patriot Act", and besides, there isn't any paperwork on it anyway!

10 – BARACK H. OBAMA 2009 - (PRESIDENT 44 & CONGRESSES 111 THROUGH 112)

"Oh, you should have seen the look on Waternoose's face when that wall went up. Woo-hoo! I hope we get a copy of that tape. Hey, you all right? Come on, we did it. We got Boo home. Sure, we put the company in the toilet, and, gee, hundreds of people will be out of work now, not to mention the angry mob that'll come after us when there's no more power... but hey, at least we had a few laughs, right? "

Mike Butowski

Monsters Inc.

President Barack H. Obama, a Democrat and our 44th President, serving in the 56th presidential term. This administration began on 20 January 2009 and will run through 20 January 2013 It will encompass the 111th and 112th Congresses. The 111th Congress had Democratic majorities in both houses while the 112th had a Democratic majority in the Senate with a Republican majority in the House.

I know I am a creature of habit but lets begin with a look at President Obama's inaugural address.

President Barack Obama, Inaugural address, 20 January 2009

My fellow citizens, I stand here today humbled by the task before us, grateful for the trust you have bestowed, mindful of the sacrifices borne by our ancestors. I thank President Bush for his service to our Nation, as well as the generosity and cooperation he has shown throughout this transition.

Forty-four Americans have now taken the Presidential oath. The words have been spoken during rising tides of prosperity and the still waters of peace. Yet every so often, the oath is taken amidst gathering clouds and raging storms. At these moments, America has carried on not simply because of the skill or vision of those in high office, but because we the people have remained faithful to the ideals of our forebears and true to our founding documents.

So it has been; so it must be with this generation of Americans.

That we are in the midst of crisis is now well understood. Our Nation is at war against a far-reaching network of violence and hatred. Our economy is badly weakened, a consequence of greed and irresponsibility on the part of some, but also our collective failure to make hard choices and prepare the Nation for a new age. Homes have been lost, jobs shed, businesses shuttered. Our health care is too costly. Our schools fail too many. And each day brings further evidence that the ways we use energy strengthen our adversaries and threaten our planet.

These are the indicators of crisis, subject to data and statistics. Less measurable but no less profound is a sapping of confidence across our land, a nagging fear that America's decline is inevitable, that the next generation must lower its sights. Today I say to you that the challenges we face are real. They are serious, and they are many. They will not be met easily or in a short span of time. But know this, America: They will be met.

On this day, we gather because we have chosen hope over fear, unity of purpose over conflict and discord. On this day, we come to proclaim an end to the petty grievances and false promises, the recriminations and worn-out dogmas that for far too long have strangled our politics.

We remain a young nation, but in the words of Scripture, the time has come to set aside childish things. The time has come to reaffirm our enduring spirit, to choose our better history, to carry forward that precious gift, that noble idea passed on from generation to generation: the God-given promise that all are equal, all are free, and all deserve a chance to pursue their full measure of happiness.

In reaffirming the greatness of our Nation, we understand that greatness is never a given. It must be earned. Our journey has never been one of shortcuts or settling for less. It has not been the path for the fainthearted, for those who prefer leisure over work or seek only the pleasures of riches and fame. Rather, it has been the risk-takers, the doers, the makers of things-- some celebrated, but more often men and women obscure in their labor--who have carried us up the long, rugged path toward prosperity and freedom.

For us, they packed up their few worldly possessions and traveled across oceans in search of a new life. For us, they toiled in sweatshops and settled the West, endured the lash of the whip, and plowed the hard Earth. For us, they fought and died in places like Concord and Gettysburg, Normandy and Khe Sanh.

Time and again, these men and women struggled and sacrificed and worked 'til their hands were raw so that we might live a better life. They saw America as bigger than the sum of our individual ambitions, greater than all the differences of birth or wealth or faction.

This is the journey we continue today. We remain the most prosperous, powerful nation on Earth. Our workers are no less productive than when this crisis began. Our minds are no less inventive. Our goods and services no less needed than they were last week or last month or last year. Our capacity remains undiminished. But our time of standing pat, of protecting narrow interests and putting off unpleasant decisions, that time has surely passed. Starting today, we must pick ourselves up, dust ourselves off, and begin again the work of remaking America.

For everywhere we look, there is work to be done. The state of the economy calls for action, bold and swift, and we will act not only to create new jobs but to lay a new foundation for growth. We will build the roads and bridges, the electric grids and digital lines that feed our commerce and bind us together. We will restore science to its rightful place and wield technology's wonders to raise health care's quality and lower its cost. We will harness the sun and the winds and the soil to fuel our cars and run our factories. And we will transform our schools and colleges and universities to meet the demands of a new age. All this we can do. All this we will do.

Now, there are some who question the scale of our ambitions, who suggest that our system cannot tolerate too many big plans. Their memories are short, for they have forgotten what this country has already done, what free men and women can achieve when imagination is joined to common purpose and necessity to courage.

What the cynics fail to understand is that the ground has shifted beneath them, that the stale political arguments that have consumed us for so long no longer apply. The question we ask today is not whether our Government is too big or too small, but whether it works; whether it helps families find jobs at a decent wage, care they can afford, a retirement that is dignified. Where the answer is yes, we intend to move forward. Where the answer is no, programs will end. And those of us who manage the public's dollars will be held to account to spend wisely, reform bad habits, and do our business in the light of day, because only then can we restore the vital trust between a people and their government.

Nor is the question before us whether the market is a force for good or ill. Its power to generate wealth and expand freedom is unmatched. But this crisis has reminded us that without a watchful eye, the market can spin out of control. The Nation cannot prosper long when it favors only the prosperous. The success of our economy has always depended not just on the size of our gross domestic product, but on the reach of our prosperity, on our ability to extend opportunity to every willing heart, not out of charity, but because it is the surest route to our common good.

As for our common defense, we reject as false the choice between our safety and our ideals. Our Founding Fathers, faced with perils that we can scarcely imagine, drafted a charter to assure the rule of law and the rights of man, a charter expanded by the blood of generations. Those ideals still light the world, and we will not give them up for expedience's sake. And so to all the other peoples and governments who are watching today, from the grandest capitals to the small village where my father was born, know that America is a friend of each nation and every man, woman, and child who seeks a future of peace and dignity, and we are ready to lead once more.

Recall that earlier generations faced down fascism and communism not just with missiles and tanks but with sturdy alliances and enduring convictions. They understood that our power alone cannot protect us, nor does it entitle us to do as we please. Instead, they knew that our power grows through its prudent use. Our security emanates from the justness of our cause, the force of our example, the tempering qualities of humility and restraint.

We are the keepers of this legacy. Guided by these principles once more, we can meet those new threats that demand even greater effort, even greater cooperation and understanding between nations. We will begin to responsibly leave Iraq to its people and forge a hard-earned peace in Afghanistan. With old friends and former foes, we will work tirelessly to lessen the nuclear threat and roll back the specter of a warming planet. We will not apologize for our way of life, nor will we waver in its defense. And for those who seek to advance their aims by inducing terror and slaughtering innocents, we say to you now that our spirit is stronger and cannot be broken. You cannot outlast us, and we will defeat you.

For we know that our patchwork heritage is a strength, not a weakness. We are a nation of Christians and Muslims, Jews and Hindus and nonbelievers. We are shaped by every language and culture, drawn from every end of this Earth. And because we have tasted the bitter swill of civil war and segregation and emerged from that dark chapter stronger and more united, we cannot help but believe that the old hatreds shall someday pass, that the lines of tribe shall soon dissolve; that as the world grows smaller, our common humanity shall reveal itself, and that America must play its role in ushering in a new era of peace.

To the Muslim world, we seek a new way forward based on mutual interest and mutual respect. To those leaders around the globe who seek to sow conflict or blame their society's ills on the West, know that your people will judge you on what you can build, not what you destroy. To those who cling to power through corruption and deceit and the silencing of dissent, know that you are on the wrong side of history, but that we will extend a hand if you are willing to unclench your fist.

To the people of poor nations, we pledge to work alongside you to make your farms flourish and let clean waters flow, to nourish starved bodies and feed hungry minds. And to those nations like ours that enjoy relative plenty, we say we can no longer afford indifference to suffering outside our borders, nor can we consume the world's resources without regard to effect, for the world has changed, and we must change with it.

As we consider the road that unfolds before us, we remember with humble gratitude those brave Americans who, at this very hour, patrol far-off deserts and distant mountains. They have something to tell us today, just as the fallen heroes who lie in Arlington whisper through the ages. We honor them not only because they are guardians of our liberty, but because they embody the spirit of service, a willingness to find meaning in something greater than themselves. And yet at this moment, a moment that will define a generation, it is precisely this spirit that must inhabit us all.

For as much as Government can do and must do, it is ultimately the faith and determination of the American people upon which this Nation relies. It is the kindness to take in a stranger when the levees break, the selflessness of workers who would rather cut their hours than see a friend lose their job, which sees us through our darkest hours. It is the firefighter's courage to storm a stairway filled with smoke, but also a parent's willingness to nurture a child, that finally decides our fate.

Our challenges may be new. The instruments with which we meet them may be new. But those values upon which our success depends--honesty and hard work, courage and fair play, tolerance and curiosity, loyalty and patriotism-- these things are old. These things are true. They have been the quiet force of progress throughout our history. What is demanded then is a return to these truths. What is required of us now is a new era of responsibility, a recognition on the part of every American that we have duties to ourselves, our Nation, and the world. Duties that we do not grudgingly accept but, rather, seize gladly, firm in the knowledge that there is nothing so satisfying to the spirit, so defining of our character, than giving our all to a difficult task.

This is the price and the promise of citizenship. This is the source of our confidence, the knowledge that God calls on us to shape an uncertain destiny. This is the meaning of our liberty and our creed; why men and women and children of every race and every faith can join in celebration across this magnificent Mall, and why a man whose father less than 60 years ago might not have been served at a local restaurant can now stand before you to take a most sacred oath.

So let us mark this day with remembrance of who we are and how far we have traveled. In the year of America's birth, in the coldest of months, a small band of patriots huddled by dying campfires on the shores of an icy river. The Capital was abandoned. The enemy was advancing. The snow was stained with blood. At a moment when the outcome of our Revolution was most in doubt, the Father of our Nation ordered these words be read to the people:

"Let it be told to the future world . . . that in the depth of winter, when nothing but hope and virtue could survive . . . that the city and the country, alarmed at one common danger, came forth to meet [it]."

America, in the face of our common dangers, in this winter of our hardship, let us remember these timeless words. With hope and virtue, let us brave once more the icy currents and endure what storms may come. Let it be said by our children's children that when we were tested, we refused to let this journey end; that we did not turn back, nor did we falter. And with eyes fixed on the horizon and God's grace upon us, we carried forth that great gift of freedom and delivered it safely to future generations.

Thank you. God bless you, and God bless the United States of America.

President Barack Obama, Inaugural address, 20 January 2009

President Obama did not mention the national debt in this address. He did mention difficult choices and the like, so lets see how this administration is doing. 2010, the first fiscal year for this administration is the only data point we have as of this writing.

Fiscal Year	Total Debt	Change	% Change
2009	$11,909,829,003,511.70		
2010	$13,561,623,030,891.80	$1,651,794,027,380.10	13.87%
Total		$1,651,794,027,380.10	13.87%

Well, not a very good start to this administration either. The slide into truly unprecedented amounts of debt continues. If this type of number continues for a year or 2 President Obama will be destined to become one of our largest borrowers in history.

As for our per year average:

Years of Existence	Total Debt	Total Change	Per Year Average Increase
1	$75,463,476.52		
220	$11,909,829,003,511.70	$11,909,753,540,035.20	$54,135,586,379.60
221	$13,561,623,030,891.80	$1,651,794,027,380.10	$61,364,810,094.53
	Percentage Change In	The per year Average	13.35%

Well President 44 only has 1 data point to plot so I believe it would be premature to add this administration to our tally just yet.

11 – ADDING IT ALL UP;
PARTY VS. PARTY

"No, Pinky. Never use two drops of the formula. It would cause a reaction on the molecular level that is completely unpredictable."

The Brain

Pinky and the Brain

If you remember when it all began for the Constitutional United States government we finished our 1ˢᵗ fiscal year at $75,463,476.52. Here we are 221 fiscal years later and that number stands at $13,561,623,030,891.80. Just for a little perspective on this. Since the beginning of President Carter's administration we have only seen one fiscal year in which our **daily average borrowing** has been below that original number from the end of our 1ˢᵗ fiscal year.

Yes, you really read that correctly. We now borrow more money in a **day, each and every day**, than President Washington's administration reported at the end of the 1ˢᵗ fiscal **YEAR**. The one nearest that mark is fiscal year 2000 from the administration of President Clinton. Keep in mind, that first fiscal year debt was made up of all the debt that had been accumulated under the 13 years our nation was governed under the auspices of the government created by the Articles of Confederation, as well as the first 20 months of the constitutionally based United States of America.

By the way, we aren't talking a few dollars more. It's usually a lot more. For example, lets look at the average daily borrowing that occurred during the administration of President Reagan. Once again, before you start sending me hate mail, hear me out. There is a reason that President Reagan was chosen for this little demonstration.

What, oh you want to know what that reason is? Why didn't you say so? Are ya ready, cause here it comes. Among the 6 Presidents that I have identified as the "modern" Presidents, 3 Democrats and 3 Republicans, symmetrical don't ya think, President Reagan is in a class all his own when it comes to the percentage increase to the national debt. President Reagan's 8 years is equivalent to 2,920 days. For each of those 2,920 days the United States borrowed $636,841,082.26. Ya know seeing it written like that doesn't quite do it justice. Try this on for size.

636 Million
841 Thousand
082 Dollars
and 26 Cents.

Per Day.... For 8 consecutive years!

And even though President Reagan is the clear leader on a percentage increase basis, on the real dollar scale his administration looks like complete amateurs when compared to President George W. Bush's 8 years, and if President Obama continues on current trajectory he will crush them both!

So what the heck has happened? When did whatever the heck happened, well, happen? We haven't come this far to leave those questions unanswered, have we? So lets get to it.

As we watched our table building through the years we have already determined that there is effectively no difference in the party performance against the national debt based upon the party affiliation of the President over the course of the entire history of our constitutionally based government.

Administration	Increased Debt	Decreased Debt	Party Totals
Democrat	15	6	21
Republican	15	7	22
Other	6	6	12
Total	36	19	55

They really could not be very much closer. The Republicans have 1 more in the decreasing column, however they also have 1 more total administration.

If you remember I defined the beginning of the Democratic party as the election of President Andrew Jackson. A point which I am sure the Democrats will object to because it places President Thomas Jefferson in the other category. While I have my reasons, first among them is the fact that I don't believe President Jefferson would identify with either of our current parties and would probably be starting another party instead, debating this point is no longer an issue. Back to the whole, he who writes the book makes the decisions.

So, lets look back and see where we were up to the election of the first Democrat, President Andrew Jackson, for the 11th presidential term. For the 10 terms preceding the first term for President Jackson, 4 had increased the debt while 6 had decreased it. Now that is a pretty good ratio. For every 2 that increase the debt, for whatever reason, you have 3 in relative short order decreasing it. That is a general downward trend, and indicates an understanding that a national debt must be handled responsibly. Perhaps they spent a lot of time blaming each other, just as we do today. However, they were obviously mature enough to raise themselves out of the elementary school playground attitude and do what needed to be done. Namely reduce the national debt, regardless of whose fault it was.

Now at this point, while there have been parties, they have been very transient. Forming, dissolving, forming, dissolving and so forth. We have seen the Federalist, who no longer exist, the Democratic-Republicans, who now no longer exist. Now we have the Democrats organized around President Jackson, and a number of other parties most notable the Whigs. So lets take a look at what happens from now until the coalescence of the Republican party with the election of President Lincoln.

This span includes 8 presidential terms. This period was not as friendly to the debt reduction cause when judged by the ratio of administrations reducing verses increasing the debt, with 5 increasing and 3 decreasing. However, it bears remembering that the administration that began this period, President Andrew Jackson, effectively retired the national debt. So it seems to me that this period also reflects a generally responsible stewardship of this nation's finances.

We are now through 18 presidential terms and those 18 administrations are exactly split with 9 increasing and 9 decreasing the national debt. Now anyone who wants to try to rationalize out of control debt by any administration should remember this. These first 18 administrations assumed all of the debt accumulated by the first government, which included the debt to fund the Revolutionary War, create our 2nd form of government from scratch, then the War of 1812. At the time of President Washington's first inauguration the nation consisted of 13 states. At the time of President Lincoln's inauguration the nation consisted of 34 states. There was the panic of 1819, the panic and depression of 1832, the panic and depression of 1836, the panic of 1837, the depression of 1837 through 1843, and the panic of 1857.

These are but a few of the reasons why, in the very beginning of this book, I said our goal was to strip away all extenuating circumstances. Just as surely as the Republicans and Democrats of today can blame all of our problems on each other, the weather, the rich, the poor, the war, Islam, liberalism, conservatism, etc. etc. etc. I think you get the point! These administrations had plenty to blame, had they decided to borrow their way to prosperity, yet they did not do it. Instead, they dealt with the situations with which they were faced and did so in a financially responsible manner.

Now lets move on, and take a look at the terms from the election of President Lincoln up to the election of President Franklin Roosevelt. This time period covers 18 presidential terms, and it was during this period when our nations politics seem to form up around the current 2 party system, major parties that is. If you remember at the time of President Lincoln's inauguration we have had 18 previous presidential terms, and those 18 are evenly split with 9 increasing the debt, and 9 decreasing the debt, including President Jackson's temporarily retiring the debt altogether.

Well terms 19 through 36 resulted in an even split, 18 increasing and 18 decreasing the debt. The splits by party were as follows; Democrats 6 increasing and 5 decreasing, Republicans 6 increasing and 7 decreasing, Other 6 increasing and 6 decreasing. We are up to the beginning of 1933 and we are still at an even split on debt performance. Neither party is showing any substantial proclivity towards reducing the debt in greater proportion than the other, but as a system of government it is all working out pretty well to this point in history. We have one run up the debt, again for whatever reason, and then we will have 1 pay the debt down at least somewhat. Now we are not seeing the debt being completely retired as with President Jackson, but I feel very comfortable with the opinion that it is well in hand, and the trend, at this point in our history, is not a source of concern.

Now we will look at the period from the inauguration of President Franklin Roosevelt to the end of President Ford's administration, 11 presidential terms. If you remember each grouping of presidential terms we have looked at so far had at worst an even split between the number of administrations increasing the national debt versus those decreasing the national debt. Oh if we could only be so lucky again. In the preceding paragraph we listed the numbers by party through the first 36 presidential terms and I have some good news, we only have half as much work to do this time to accomplish the same task.

Why whatever do you mean? Thanks for asking. What I mean by that is this. Simply look at the numbers for each party that decreased the debt through the first 36 terms and you have the number by party of administrations decreasing the debt through 47 presidential terms. That's right, not ONE administration reduced the national debt by even $1.00, from 1933 through the end of 1976. To be precise the last administration to reduce the national debt was President Calvin Coolidge, a Republican, serving in the 35th presidential term.

This period was followed by the election of President Jimmy Carter, a Democrat, presiding over a 42.7% increase. President Ronald Reagan, a Republican, presiding over a 82.7 % increase in term 1, a 56.7% increase in term 2, and a 8 year total increase of 186%. Then we elected President

George H. W. Bush, a Republican, who presided over a 54.3% increase. President William J. Clinton, a Democrat, presided over a 22.7% increase in term 1, a 7.3% increase in term 2, and a 8 year total increase of 31.6%. President George W. Bush, a Republican, presiding over a 36.6% increase in term 1, a 50.1% increase in term 2, and a 8 year total increase of 105%. Lastly we have President Barack Obama, a Democrat, presiding over a single fiscal year to the date of this writing with a 13.8% increase.

As to the central question of this entire book, is there a dime's difference in our two major political parties here in the early 21st century. I submit to you the answer to that question is a resounding NO! Not only is there little if any difference in them in the early 21st century, but I submit to you, there has never been a great deal of difference between them. Prior to the 1930's both parties performed in a manner that would indicate a general understanding that the national debt had to be handled responsibly and maintained at modest levels. Then beginning in the 1930's it is equally clear that both parties performed in a manner that would indicate a loss of respect for the need to restrain the national debt to modest levels.

Then beginning in 1976 it seems that increasing the national debt became a game of one upmanship, which I will say the Republicans are winning handily.

Unfortunately, both parties have administrations in their unquestioned legacies that demonstrate strong fiscal discipline. Namely President Andrew Jackson, a Democrat, effectively retired the national debt. Likewise President Calvin Coolidge, a Republican, reduced the national debt by over 30% in a single 4 year term.

Why then have both parties strayed so very far from the path that was working so very well? History, our history, the history of the end of our 1st form of government, the history of the beginning of our 2nd and still current form of government speak to us clearly that debt uncontrolled will end your government! Why then, does it seem that no one is listening?

How is it that, from President George Washington in 1789 through President Calvin Coolidge in 1929 and regardless of party affiliation, our presidents understood this fundamental lesson and governed or lead in effective accordance. Then just as cleanly as turning off a light switch from 1930 through today not one, not one regardless of party affiliation, of our Presidents has listened, nor led effectively, when considering the national debt and those very lessons delineated above.

At this point I would like to harken back to some things President George Washington had to say in his farewell address.

"All obstructions to the execution of the laws, all combinations and associations, under whatever plausible character, with the real design to direct, control, counteract, or awe the regular deliberation and action of the constituted authorities, are destructive of this fundamental principle, and of fatal tendency. They serve to organize faction, to give it an artificial and extraordinary force; to put, in the place of the delegated will of the nation the will of a party, often a small but artful and enterprising minority of the community; and, according to the alternate triumphs of different parties, to make the public administration the mirror of the ill-concerted and incongruous projects of faction, rather than the organ of consistent and wholesome plans digested by common counsels and modified by mutual interests.

However combinations or associations of the above description may now and then answer popular ends, they are likely, in the course of time and things, to become potent engines, by which cunning, ambitious, and unprincipled men will be enabled to subvert the power of the people and to usurp for themselves the reins of government, destroying afterwards the very engines which have lifted them to unjust dominion. "

Is that quote anything less than a perfect description of what we have just watched develop over the course of all these chapters, and all these tables, and all these dates, covering the history of our constitutional government? Is it not apparent that the, destruction of the engines which have lifted them to unjust dominion, is undeniably manifesting itself right before our very eyes?

"Baby what a big surprise, right before my very eyes" Sorry about that, but you have to admit that is a really good song. Back to business.

It appears as though President Washington was in fact able to predict the consequences of adding 2 drops of the formula!

Charles F. Stamper

12 – A WAY FORWARD;
IN MY OPINION

"Heavily armed, blood thirsty pirates against the Harvey family?
Guys, it would take a miracle"

Martin Harvey

Captain Ron

So where do we go from here? Well there is a show on HGTV called "House Hunter's International" and they all seem to think Costa Rica is nice this time of year. But, since that probably only appeals to a very few people who, one have a lot of money, and two don't mind being ex patriots, I think we will look for a few other answers before we get quite that drastic.

One of the options that has been floated off and on for the past few years is that of a balanced budget amendment to the constitution. Well might as well get straight to the point here, I don't think that this idea will work at all, and here are just a few reasons for that opinion. First, if we have expenditures that can be "off budget" then we could have a balanced budget submitted each and every year and the national debt could still continue to climb unabated.

Secondly, anyone who lives in a city of any size has already heard or felt this one I'm sure. When politicians are forced to cut spending they tend to trim it from those departments that actually serve a purpose to civil society. Such as police departments, fire departments, refuse collection, to name a popular few. While leaving the infamous bridges to nowhere fully funded. Curiously, you never hear anything about cutting the salaries, or in most cases the guaranteed annual "cost of living" raises of elected officials who have led, or their predecessors have led, their particular unit of government into it's state of financial insolvency.

Thirdly, I believe this to be indicative of a desperate last hope of a tired and desperate people, too exhausted to live up to the expectation placed upon us by the constitution. The truth of the matter is this, we the people have all the power we need to control our government right now, as written. The truth also is that it requires effort, time, energy, imagination, and yes even a little money to act upon the power we have. I do not believe that, if we hope to survive as a nation that we at least vaguely recognize, we can abdicate our responsibility to manage our elected officials through the electoral process to the automation of a balanced budget amendment. If you do a little studying of the constitution I think you will reach the same conclusion. Our government is operating well outside the bounds of the constitution as it is written right now, and has been doing so for a considerable time. A balanced budget amendment would simply give them something else to ignore.

Lastly, I believe this would be just another effort to deal with a symptom of our national political disease, as opposed to curing our national political disease. This book has concentrated on the executive of our nation, and the party affiliation of that executive. However, it certainly isn't lost on the author, me, that we have a legislative and judicial branch of government as well. For a moment lets take a look at the "leadership" of the current United States Senate.

First, lets look at the Senate majority leader, from Nevada, Democrat Senator Harry Reid. Senator Reid was elected to the Senate for the first time in 1986 and has been returned by his states electorate ever since. When Senator Reid first went to Washington D.C. as a senator the national debt at the end of fiscal 1986 stood at $2,125,302,616,658.42, as of this writing, fiscal 2010 is the last year for which we have official data and it reflects a national debt of $13,561,623,030,891.79. That is an increase of $11,436,320,414,233.37 in his time in office to date. That is a percentage increase of 538%.

Secondly, lets look at the Senate minority leader, from my own state of Kentucky, Republican Senator Mitch McConnell. Senator McConnell was elected to the Senate for the first time in 1984 and has been returned by his states electorate ever since. When Senator McConnell first went to Washington D. C. as a senator the national debt at the end of fiscal 1984 stood at $1,572,266,000,000.00, as of this writing fiscal 2010 is the last year for which we have official data and it reflects a national debt of $13,561,623,030,891.79. That is an increase of $11,989,357,030,891.79 in his time in office to date. That is a percentage increase of 762%.

The electorate of Senator Reid has had the opportunity to reintroduce him to civilian life 4 times and has failed to do so even as the national debt spiraled out of control. The electorate of Senator McConnell has had the opportunity to reintroduce him to civilian life 4 times and has failed to do so even as the national debt spiraled out of control. Do you see a common theme here? One Democrat, one Republican, turning a position envisioned as one of a "citizen legislator" into a very lucrative career, all the while building a work history that would get you fired from a private sector company in 30 days or less. Please remember that one of the primary purposes of the legislative branch as outlined in the constitution is stewardship of the nations finances. All of this, with the blessing of the voting, key word here is voting, public.

Please don't think I'm picking on these 2 states, all 50 are guilty of the same "I can't stand Congress but "MY" Congressman is just fine" voting practice. How else is one to explain Congress' dismal approval rating. Yet, an awful lot of the senators and representatives have been in Washington D. C. for a very, very long time. Oops, I just noticed we have taken a turn into a subject for another book, which I am currently working on by the way, so I'll leave this discussion here for now.

Well I've already told you a little bit about what will not work and why, at least, in my opinion. Since the title of this chapter is "A Way Forward; In My Opinion" I guess we should get to it.

President Millard Fillmore once gave this somewhat bleak assessment of what might be needed to save the United States, "May God save the country, for it is evident that the people will not." While I can certainly understand the sentiment I am not inclined to agree quite yet. In truth the only thing that can save this nation is "We The People". We must become active, engaged, and learned on the issues of the day. We must keep a watchful eye on our Congress men and women, our Presidents, and even our supreme court justices. We must bring our federal government, back to a stable financial footing, and back within the boundaries established in the constitution. As a baseline if nothing else. Then, as inadequacies are identified, the Constitution provides a tool for correcting such inadequacies. The tool is the amendment process. Above all else we must vote. Everyone must vote.

Now I realize that you are probably thinking, there isn't much new in the paragraph above. Anybody who is writing or talking about politics and any attempt to solve some of the issues with our politics is saying something that sounds very similar. However, they offer no help, or ideas on how to accomplish such things in our already busy, worried, harried lives. Where would we ever find the time, the energy, the money, and why bother voting it won't really make a difference anyway, right? Right.

First things first. By the title of this book and the research we have just been through I feel it is pretty obvious that my primary concern for the future of this nation is the national debt. I am not alone in my concern for this issue. As evidence, I offer the following thought from President Thomas Jefferson:

"I ... place economy among the first and most important of republican virtues, and public debt as the greatest of dangers to be feared... And to preserve (our) independence, we must not let our rulers load us with perpetual debt. We must make our election between economy and liberty, or profusion and servitude. "

Further, I believe the condition of the national debt is merely a symptom of a very different political disease. So what is the disease you ask? I believe it to be the two party system. Let's see if we can find a way to treat the disease and in so doing improve or eliminate the symptom of the national debt.

Everyone, that talks and writes about these things for a living, couldn't stop talking about the "message" that voters had sent to the politicians with the election of 2008. Then with the election of 2010 and the Republican/tea party surge, those same people started talking about the "message" that the voters had sent to the politicians with that election. Meanwhile, here in Georgetown, KY and thousands of other cities, towns, and rural areas around this nation nothing changed. The debt continues to climb unabated, unemployment continues to rise, the Democrats blame the Republicans, the Republicans blame the Democrats. Yet, one of the things I recommended was that we all must vote. Now you are reading this and going oh yeah, right, voting has really helped in the past why would it help now. I hope you are ready for the answer cause here it comes.

First, in the sports world, especially in college football, you hear coaches talking about approaching a season as a series of 1 game seasons. I suggest that we as voters should look at our individual votes as 1 voter elections. When you go into that booth pretend you are the only person voting and your one vote will decide the entire issue. In reality that is exactly what happens, in the case of President, tens of millions, of one person, one vote elections. We just loose site of that fact when all those votes are tallied together and reported.

Secondly, if you we want to send an effective message, what we the people, the voting public must do, beginning with the 2012 elections, is fill every single office that is being chosen with an individual that is not affiliated with either the Democrats nor the Republicans. Representatives, Senators, and yes even the President. Now upon first reading, a lot of people are going to think, "OK this guy is crazy, doesn't he realize how important these positions really are to the nation and even the world. We can't replace people who know what they are doing with just anybody, in mass".

Fair enough, I have a couple of answers to that one. Here is the first. Currently this nation is financially insolvent, we are involved in 2 active shooting wars each over 10 years in duration, we currently live with something called the Patriot Act which among other things allows a number of the individual liberties of all Americans to be usurped. We have bridges on major roads that are being closed because they are unsafe and we have no money to fix them, we have the Chinese government feeling it necessary to give us financial advice as we owe them so much money, Social Security is supposedly bankrupt, medicare as well, the constitutionally required U.S.

Postal Service is nearing bankruptcy. The list truly goes on and on and on, ad infinitum.

These are just a few of the results of the experts, the ruling class, the Democrats and the Republicans, the ones you expect me to believe we can't relieve of their public responsibilities because it would be too dangerous? That sounds a lot like some private too large to fail company getting tax payer funded bailouts only to pay huge bonuses to those that led them to bankruptcy in the first place and, with a straight face I might add, justify those bonuses by saying they have to keep the best talent. I suppose lesser talent might not have got them to bankruptcy nearly as quickly as they wanted to get there or something.

If these are the experts I say give me a few amateurs. Go to the polls, vote, if the only choices you have for a given race are 1 Democrat and 1 Republican, then write someone in. I would even argue that you could write in another Democrat or Republican and the "message" to the 2 parties would be equally as loud. For example I am of the opinion that, of all the people who have announced that they are running or are public about considering running, Ron Paul is the only one that seems to have any viable understanding of where we actually are as a nation, yet he has little if any chance of actually becoming the official Republican nominee. As for the Democrats, President Obama is nearly certain to go unopposed to the nomination and a run for re-election. Assuming I am correct in both cases consider a write in vote for Ron Paul.

The same goes for the Senate races and the races for the House of Representatives. Talk to your family and friends, identify some one in your Congressional district, ask them if they were to be elected in a write in campaign would they be willing to serve their country for 2 years as a representative, or 6 years as a senator. Assuming they say yes write a letter to the editor of every newspaper in the appropriate geography announcing the write in effort. Offer to serve yourself in the manner described above. As a matter of fact, I will offer my name, right now, for the House of Representatives in the 6th district of Kentucky. If elected I will serve the term. I'm not going to ask any of you to do something I'm not willing to do myself.

Now before you go off and call the guys with the white jackets to come get me, the whole thing about writing people in, is mostly but not entirely in jest, although it would be absolutely hilarious if you think about it. What I'm suggesting is that we begin to view holding elected office at any level of government, be it federal , state, or local as an opportunity to sacrifice and serve our country for a limited period of time and then return to private life. Our government desperately needs, must be open to, participation from all Americans. That you and I, your neighbor and mine, are completely capable of handling the responsibilities of these offices, I have absolutely no doubt. In short, I have seen, and am seeing, in my working life, incredibly talented people with a lot to offer being largely ignored by managers, and executives at companies who then wonder aloud why employee moral is low and quality just isn't what it used to be. Then I hear the political talking heads speaking of qualifications, talent, and experience of this or that candidate who, to a person, has been in or intimately associated with the government that has driven this nation closer to bankruptcy than it has been since the 1780s at the end of our first government formed under the Articles of Confederation. I truly believe in a very widely dispersed body of talent and intelligence in this nation. I don't believe that any particular group of people have anything close to a monopoly on the necessary skill set to govern our cities, states, and yes even our nation. I'm suggesting also that we begin immediately to assist all those who have turned elected office into careers, by re-introducing them, each and every one, to private life. Replacing them with, teachers who would rather be teaching. Farmers who would rather be farming. Factory workers who would rather be in the factory. Homemakers who would rather be in the home, and will return to their private lives eagerly after service of 1 or 2 terms in a given office.

In the 1960s President John F. Kennedy said, "Ask not what your country can do for you, but what you can do for you country", in the short span of 20 years we go from that to this from President Ronald Reagan in the 1980s, "Are you better off now than you were 4 years ago?". Notice the difference, one calls the individual to sacrifice for something larger than ones self, namely the nation. The second focuses exclusively on the individual, forget everyone else for a moment how are you doing. I believe it is once again time to echo the sentiment of President Kennedy in asking, "What can you do for your country". Please consider public service for a short time in elected office.

Another great idea, I can say that because it's my idea, would be to identify the candidate who has raised the largest amount of money for their campaign and then vote for someone, anyone, else. Yes, you read that correctly. It seems widely accepted that big money corrupts the political process. Some people may disagree but they would be wrong. So what do we do about the big money, I suggest we make it a recipe for losing elections. No legislation, no new laws, no new rules, no public financing of campaigns. Instead we should force disclosure, and punish those who sell their soul expecting to then use those massive sums of money to indirectly, that's my optimistic nature coming out, purchase elections. Which they then, of course, use the office to more than repay those who paid out the most. If the largest money collectors begin to lose elections in mass, that will change very quickly.

As for those of you that say, well how would we know what the candidates stand for if they can't purchase air time for TV commercials and the like? That too is quite easily resolved. Ever heard of the nightly news, CNN, CBS, NBC, ABC, Fox News, newspapers, the internet, PBS, CSPAN, radio the list literally goes on and on and on. Staffs and so called grass roots organizations could be made up of volunteers. Here is a novel idea, candidates could write their own speeches, instead of paying professional speech writers and political consultants. Hey, how about this, most officials tend to run for re-election, how about we, the voting public, look into the record of incumbents on our own. It really isn't that hard to do.

In case your wondering why I haven't recommended you stop contributing to political campaigns, well that would be because I haven't gotten to it until now. Now you should certainly be aware that there is a group of people and organizations in this country that are actually referred to as the political donor class. This donor class roughly represents the top 0.5% of Americans ranked by wealth and the largest of corporations which are largely owned and operated by, you guessed it, the top 0.5% of Americans. While I am sure that each of you will agree with me and stop all political giving as of now, it will not completely solve the problem with today's astronomical campaign coffers. However, anything we can do in this regard will certainly help. While money may not be the root of all evil, it certainly makes very potent fertilizer.

Next, change your voter registration. Become a truly independent voter. As I mentioned in the prologue, the form I received at my county clerks office only listed Republican, Democrat, and other, so technically I am an other. If the roles of registered Democrats and Republicans start dropping by 10 or 20% per month for a couple of months "change you can believe in" will begin immediately. Also here in Kentucky we actually have a button in the voting booth, actually there are 2 buttons. One says vote for all Democrats and one says vote for all Republicans. Why? If your state has something similar, or you have heard any logical reason this should be the case, please use the contact form at www.breathittpublishing.com and let us know about it.

One more thing that I have done is to actually purchase 5 copies of the book "The Constitution of the United States of America, with all of the

Amendments; The Declaration of Independence; and The Articles of Confederation" which in the interest of full disclosure, I publish, and sent them to the President, Vice-President, both of my Senators, and my Representative. Cost me $35.00 plus shipping, but maybe they will get the hint that I would at least like for them to read it even if they have no intention of following it. Although, I may well be on the no fly list after that. If you would like to do the same, the book is available at www.breathittpublishing.com and there is a discount code in the back of this book good for 10% off, so you will be able to do it cheaper than I did. If about a million of us could do this, maybe they will get the point. If not, I'll be rich, and well lets not forget Costa Rica!

In conclusion, I would like to offer this final plea. In the discipline of psychology you will occasionally encounter a person called an enabler. More colloquially, I have heard it described as someone who will "give a drunk a drink". The idea is basically this. If you decide to knowingly provide access to a particular persons vice, when they would otherwise have no access to it, at some point you become at least partially responsible for their misbehavior. Reason being, that you enabled, or assisted in making the otherwise impossible, possible. If you remember earlier in this chapter I asked that each of us begin to view our elections not as a single huge event in which one vote could get eaten up and become meaningless. But rather as a series of 10's of millions of single voter, single vote contests. I am now asking each of you to, when you step into that voting both and close the curtain and begin to make your choices for each and every race at issue, ask yourself this question. "Am I, giving a drunk a drink?"

Lest we not forget, as we learned on the title page of this the last chapter, of this our first, of what I hope to be many, conversations;

"Guys, it would take a miracle".

Charles F. Stamper

Appendix 1 – The Constitution of the United States of America

Article I - The Legislative Branch

Section 1 - The Legislature

All legislative Powers herein granted shall be vested in a Congress of the United States, which shall consist of a Senate and House of Representatives.

Section 2 - The House

The House of Representatives shall be composed of Members chosen every second Year by the People of the several States, and the Electors in each State shall have the Qualifications requisite for Electors of the most numerous Branch of the State Legislature.

No Person shall be a Representative who shall not have attained to the Age of twenty five Years, and been seven Years a Citizen of the United States, and who shall not, when elected, be an Inhabitant of that State in which he shall be chosen.

(Representatives and direct Taxes shall be apportioned among the several States which may be included within this Union, according to their respective Numbers, which shall be determined by adding to the whole Number of free Persons, including those bound to Service for a Term of Years, and excluding Indians not taxed, three fifths of all other Persons.) **(The previous sentence in parentheses was modified by the 14th Amendment, section 2.)** The actual Enumeration shall be made within three Years after the first Meeting of the Congress of the United States, and within every subsequent Term of ten Years, in such Manner as they shall by Law direct.

The Number of Representatives shall not exceed one for every thirty Thousand, but each State shall have at Least one Representative; and until such enumeration shall be made, the State of New Hampshire shall be entitled to chuse three, Massachusetts eight, Rhode Island and Providence Plantations one, Connecticut five, New York six, New Jersey four, Pennsylvania eight, Delaware one, Maryland six, Virginia ten, North Carolina five, South Carolina five and Georgia three.

When vacancies happen in the Representation from any State, the Executive Authority thereof shall issue Writs of Election to fill such Vacancies.

The House of Representatives shall chuse their Speaker and other Officers; and shall have the sole Power of Impeachment.

Section 3 - The Senate

The Senate of the United States shall be composed of two Senators from each State, *(chosen by the Legislature thereof,)* **(The preceding words in parentheses superseded by 17th Amendment, section 1.)** for six Years; and each Senator shall have one Vote.

Immediately after they shall be assembled in Consequence of the first Election, they shall be divided as equally as may be into three Classes. The Seats of the Senators of the first Class shall be vacated at the Expiration of the second Year, of the second Class at the Expiration of the fourth Year, and of the third Class at the Expiration of the sixth Year, so that one third may be chosen every second Year; *(and if Vacancies happen by Resignation, or otherwise, during the Recess of the Legislature of any State, the Executive thereof may make temporary Appointments until the next Meeting of the Legislature, which shall then fill such Vacancies.)* **(The preceding words in parentheses were superseded by the 17th Amendment, section 2.)**

No person shall be a Senator who shall not have attained to the Age of thirty Years, and been nine Years a Citizen of the United States, and who shall not, when elected, be an Inhabitant of that State for which he shall be chosen.

The Vice President of the United States shall be President of the Senate, but shall have no Vote, unless they be equally divided.

The Senate shall chuse their other Officers, and also a President pro tempore, in the absence of the Vice President, or when he shall exercise the Office of President of the United States.

The Senate shall have the sole Power to try all Impeachments. When sitting for that Purpose, they shall be on Oath or Affirmation. When the President of the United States is tried, the Chief Justice shall preside: And no Person shall be convicted without the Concurrence of two thirds of the Members present.

Judgment in Cases of Impeachment shall not extend further than to removal from Office, and disqualification to hold and enjoy any Office of honor, Trust or Profit under the United States: but the Party convicted shall nevertheless be liable and subject to Indictment, Trial, Judgment and Punishment, according to Law.

Section 4 - Elections, Meetings

The Times, Places and Manner of holding Elections for Senators and Representatives, shall be prescribed in each State by the Legislature thereof; but the Congress may at any time by Law make or alter such Regulations, except as to the Place of Chusing Senators.

The Congress shall assemble at least once in every Year, and such Meeting shall *(be on the first Monday in December,)* **(The preceding words in parentheses were superseded by the 20th Amendment, section 2.)** unless they shall by Law appoint a different Day.

Section 5 - Membership, Rules, Journals, Adjournment

Each House shall be the Judge of the Elections, Returns and Qualifications of its own Members, and a Majority of each shall constitute a Quorum to do Business; but a smaller number may adjourn from day to day, and may be authorized to compel the Attendance of absent Members, in such Manner, and under such Penalties as each House may provide.

Each House may determine the Rules of its Proceedings, punish its Members for disorderly Behavior, and, with the Concurrence of two-thirds, expel a Member.

Each House shall keep a Journal of its Proceedings, and from time to time publish the same, excepting such Parts as may in their Judgment require Secrecy; and the Yeas and Nays of the Members of either House on any question shall, at the Desire of one fifth of those Present, be entered on the Journal.

Neither House, during the Session of Congress, shall, without the Consent of the other, adjourn for more than three days, nor to any other Place than that in which the two Houses shall be sitting.

Section 6 – Compensation

(The Senators and Representatives shall receive a Compensation for their Services, to be ascertained by Law, and paid out of the Treasury of the United States.) **(The preceding words in parentheses were modified by the 27th Amendment.)** They shall in all Cases, except Treason, Felony and Breach of the Peace, be privileged from Arrest during their Attendance at the Session of their respective Houses, and in going to and returning from the same; and for any Speech or Debate in either House, they shall not be questioned in any other Place.

No Senator or Representative shall, during the Time for which he was elected, be appointed to any civil Office under the Authority of the United States which shall have been created, or the Emoluments whereof shall have been increased during such time; and no Person holding any Office under the United States, shall be a Member of either House during his Continuance in Office.

Section 7 - Revenue Bills, Legislative Process, Presidential Veto

All bills for raising Revenue shall originate in the House of Representatives; but the Senate may propose or concur with Amendments as on other Bills.

Every Bill which shall have passed the House of Representatives and the Senate, shall, before it become a Law, be presented to the President of the United States; If he approve he shall sign it, but if not he shall return it, with his Objections to that House in which it shall have originated, who shall enter the Objections at large on their Journal, and proceed to reconsider it. If after such Reconsideration two thirds of that House shall agree to pass the Bill, it shall be sent, together with the Objections, to the other House, by which it shall likewise be reconsidered, and if approved by two thirds of that House, it shall become a Law. But in all such Cases the Votes of both Houses shall be determined by Yeas and Nays, and the Names of the Persons voting for and against the Bill shall be entered on the Journal of each House respectively. If any Bill shall not be returned by the President within ten Days (Sundays excepted) after it shall have been presented to him, the Same shall be a Law, in like Manner as if he had signed it, unless the Congress by their Adjournment prevent its Return, in which Case it shall not be a Law.

Every Order, Resolution, or Vote to which the Concurrence of the Senate and House of Representatives may be necessary (except on a question of Adjournment) shall be presented to the

President of the United States; and before the Same shall take Effect, shall be approved by him, or being disapproved by him, shall be repassed by two thirds of the Senate and House of Representatives, according to the Rules and Limitations prescribed in the Case of a Bill.

Section 8 - Powers of Congress

The Congress shall have Power To lay and collect Taxes, Duties, Imposts and Excises, to pay the Debts and provide for the common Defence and general Welfare of the United States; but all Duties, Imposts and Excises shall be uniform throughout the United States;

To borrow money on the credit of the United States;

To regulate Commerce with foreign Nations, and among the several States, and with the Indian Tribes;

To establish an uniform Rule of Naturalization, and uniform Laws on the subject of Bankruptcies throughout the United States;

To coin Money, regulate the Value thereof, and of foreign Coin, and fix the Standard of Weights and Measures;

To provide for the Punishment of counterfeiting the Securities and current Coin of the United States;

To establish Post Offices and Post Roads;To promote the Progress of Science and useful Arts, by securing for limited Times to Authors and Inventors the exclusive Right to their respective Writings and Discoveries;

To constitute Tribunals inferior to the supreme Court;

To define and punish Piracies and Felonies committed on the high Seas, and Offenses against the Law of Nations;

To declare War, grant Letters of Marque and Reprisal, and make Rules concerning Captures on Land and Water;

To raise and support Armies, but no Appropriation of Money to that Use shall be for a longer Term than two Years;

To provide and maintain a Navy;

To make Rules for the Government and Regulation of the land and naval Forces;

To provide for calling forth the Militia to execute the Laws of the Union, suppress Insurrections and repel Invasions;

To provide for organizing, arming, and disciplining the Militia, and for governing such Part of them as may be employed in the Service of the United States, reserving to the States respectively, the Appointment of the Officers, and the Authority of training the Militia according to the discipline prescribed by Congress;

To exercise exclusive Legislation in all Cases whatsoever, over such District (not exceeding ten Miles square) as may, by Cession of particular States, and the acceptance of Congress, become the Seat of the Government of the United States, and to exercise like Authority over all Places purchased by the Consent of the Legislature of the State in which the Same shall be, for the Erection of Forts, Magazines, Arsenals, dock-Yards, and other needful Buildings; And

To make all Laws which shall be necessary and proper for carrying into Execution the foregoing Powers, and all other Powers vested by this Constitution in the Government of the United States, or in any Department or Officer thereof.

Section 9 - Limits on Congress

The Migration or Importation of such Persons as any of the States now existing shall think proper to admit, shall not be prohibited by the Congress prior to the Year one thousand eight hundred and eight, but a tax or duty may be imposed on such Importation, not exceeding ten dollars for each Person.

The privilege of the Writ of Habeas Corpus shall not be suspended, unless when in Cases of Rebellion or Invasion the public Safety may require it.

No Bill of Attainder or ex post facto Law shall be passed.

(No capitation, or other direct, Tax shall be laid, unless in Proportion to the Census or Enumeration herein before directed to be taken.) **(Section in parentheses clarified by the 16th Amendment.)**

No Tax or Duty shall be laid on Articles exported from any State.

No Preference shall be given by any Regulation of Commerce or Revenue to the Ports of one State over those of another: nor shall Vessels bound to, or from, one State, be obliged to enter, clear, or pay Duties in another.

No Money shall be drawn from the Treasury, but in Consequence of Appropriations made by Law; and a regular Statement and Account of the Receipts and Expenditures of all public Money shall be published from time to time.

No Title of Nobility shall be granted by the United States: And no Person holding any Office of Profit or Trust under them, shall, without the Consent of the Congress, accept of any present, Emolument, Office, or Title, of any kind whatever, from any King, Prince or foreign State.

Section 10 - Powers Prohibited of States

No State shall enter into any Treaty, Alliance, or Confederation; grant Letters of Marque and Reprisal; coin Money; emit Bills of Credit; make any Thing but gold and silver Coin a Tender in Payment of Debts; pass any Bill of Attainder, ex post facto Law, or Law impairing the Obligation of Contracts, or grant any Title of Nobility.

No State shall, without the Consent of the Congress, lay any Imposts or Duties on Imports or Exports, except what may be absolutely necessary for executing it's inspection Laws: and the net Produce of all Duties and Imposts, laid by any State on Imports or Exports, shall be for the Use of the

Treasury of the United States; and all such Laws shall be subject to the Revision and Controul of the Congress.

No State shall, without the Consent of Congress, lay any duty of Tonnage, keep Troops, or Ships of War in time of Peace, enter into any Agreement or Compact with another State, or with a foreign Power, or engage in War, unless actually invaded, or in such imminent Danger as will not admit of delay.

Article II - The Executive Branch

Section 1 - The President

The executive power shall be vested in a President of the United States of America. He shall hold his Office during the Term of four Years, and, together with the Vice-President chosen for the same Term, be elected, as follows:

Each State shall appoint, in such Manner as the Legislature thereof may direct, a Number of Electors, equal to the whole Number of Senators and Representatives to which the State may be entitled in the Congress: but no Senator or Representative, or Person holding an Office of Trust or Profit under the United States, shall be appointed an Elector.

(The Electors shall meet in their respective States, and vote by Ballot for two persons, of whom one at least shall not lie an Inhabitant of the same State with themselves. And they shall make a List of all the Persons voted for, and of the Number of Votes for each; which List they shall sign and certify, and transmit sealed to the Seat of the Government of the United States, directed to the President of the Senate. The President of the Senate shall, in the Presence of the Senate and House of Representatives, open all the Certificates, and the Votes shall then be counted. The Person having the greatest Number of Votes shall be the President, if such Number be a Majority of the whole Number of Electors appointed; and if there be more than one who have such Majority, and have an equal Number of Votes, then the House of Representatives shall immediately chuse by Ballot one of them for President; and if no Person have a Majority, then from the five highest on the List the said House shall in like Manner chuse the President. But in chusing the President, the Votes shall be taken by States, the Representation from each State having one Vote; a quorum for this Purpose shall consist of a Member or Members from two-thirds of the States, and a Majority of all the States shall be necessary to a Choice. In

every Case, after the Choice of the President, the Person having the greatest Number of Votes of the Electors shall be the Vice President. But if there should remain two or more who have equal Votes, the Senate shall chuse from them by Ballot the Vice-President.) **(This clause in parentheses was superseded by the 12th Amendment.)** The Congress may determine the Time of chusing the Electors, and the Day on which they shall give their Votes; which Day shall be the same throughout the United States. No person except a natural born Citizen, or a Citizen of the United States, at the time of the Adoption of this Constitution, shall be eligible to the Office of President; neither shall any Person be eligible to that Office who shall not have attained to the Age of thirty-five Years, and been fourteen Years a Resident within the United States.

(In Case of the Removal of the President from Office, or of his Death, Resignation, or Inability to discharge the Powers and Duties of the said Office, the same shall devolve on the Vice President, and the Congress may by Law provide for the Case of Removal, Death, Resignation or Inability, both of the President and Vice President, declaring what Officer shall then act as President, and such Officer shall act accordingly, until the Disability be removed, or a President shall be elected.) **(This clause in parentheses has been modified by the 20th and 25th Amendments.)**

The President shall, at stated Times, receive for his Services, a Compensation, which shall neither be increased nor diminished during the Period for which he shall have been elected, and he shall not receive within that Period any other Emolument from the United States, or any of them.

Before he enter on the Execution of his Office, he shall take the following Oath or Affirmation:

"I do solemnly swear (or affirm) that I will faithfully execute the Office of President of the United States, and will to the best of my Ability, preserve, protect and defend the Constitution of the United States."

Section 2 - Civilian Power over Military, Cabinet, Pardon Power, Appointments

The President shall be Commander in Chief of the Army and Navy of the United States, and of the Militia of the several States, when called into the actual Service of the United States; he may require the Opinion, in writing, of the principal Officer in each of the executive Departments, upon any subject relating to the Duties of their respective Offices, and he shall have Power to Grant Reprieves and Pardons for Offenses against the United States, except in Cases of Impeachment.

He shall have Power, by and with the Advice and Consent of the Senate, to make Treaties, provided two thirds of the Senators present concur; and he shall nominate, and by and with the Advice and Consent of the Senate, shall appoint Ambassadors, other public Ministers and Consuls, Judges of the supreme Court, and all other Officers of the United States, whose Appointments are not herein otherwise provided for, and which shall be established by Law: but the Congress may by Law vest the Appointment of such inferior Officers, as they think proper, in the President alone, in the Courts of Law, or in the Heads of Departments.

The President shall have Power to fill up all Vacancies that may happen during the Recess of the Senate, by granting Commissions which shall expire at the End of their next Session.

Section 3 - State of the Union, Convening Congress

He shall from time to time give to the Congress Information of the State of the Union, and recommend to their Consideration such Measures as he shall judge necessary and expedient; he may, on extraordinary Occasions, convene both Houses, or either of them, and in Case of Disagreement between them, with Respect to the Time of Adjournment, he may adjourn them to such Time as he shall think proper; he shall receive Ambassadors and other public Ministers; he shall take Care that the Laws be faithfully executed, and shall Commission all the Officers of the United States.

Section 4 – Disqualification

The President, Vice President and all civil Officers of the United States, shall be removed from Office on Impeachment for, and Conviction of, Treason, Bribery, or other high Crimes and Misdemeanors.

Article III - The Judicial Branch

Section 1 - Judicial Powers

The judicial power of the United States, shall be vested in one supreme Court, and in such inferior Courts as the Congress may from time to time ordain and establish. The Judges, both of the supreme and inferior Courts, shall hold their Offices during good Behavior, and shall, at stated Times, receive for their Services a Compensation which shall not be diminished during their Continuance in Office.

Section 2 - Trial by Jury, Original Jurisdiction, Jury Trials

(The judicial Power shall extend to all Cases, in Law and Equity, arising under this Constitution, the Laws of the United States, and Treaties made, or which shall be made, under their Authority; to all Cases affecting Ambassadors, other public Ministers and Consuls; to all Cases of admiralty and maritime Jurisdiction; to Controversies to which the United States shall be a Party; to Controversies between two or more States; between a State and Citizens of another State; between Citizens of different States; between Citizens of the same State claiming Lands under Grants of different States, and between a State, or the Citizens thereof, and foreign States, Citizens or Subjects.) **(This section in parentheses is modified by the 11th Amendment.)**

In all Cases affecting Ambassadors, other public Ministers and Consuls, and those in which a State shall be Party, the supreme Court shall have original Jurisdiction. In all the other Cases before mentioned, the supreme Court shall have appellate Jurisdiction, both as to Law and Fact, with such Exceptions, and under such Regulations as the Congress shall make.

The Trial of all Crimes, except in Cases of Impeachment, shall be by Jury; and such Trial shall be held in the State where the said Crimes shall have been committed; but when not committed within any State, the Trial shall be at such Place or Places as the Congress may by Law have directed.

Section 3 - Treason

Treason against the United States, shall consist only in levying War against them, or in adhering to their Enemies, giving them Aid and Comfort. No Person shall be convicted of Treason unless on the Testimony of two Witnesses to the same overt Act, or on Confession in open Court.

The Congress shall have power to declare the Punishment of Treason, but no Attainder of Treason shall work Corruption of Blood, or Forfeiture except during the Life of the Person attainted.

Article IV - The States

Section 1 - Each State to Honor all Others

Full Faith and Credit shall be given in each State to the public Acts, Records, and judicial Proceedings of every other State. And the Congress may by general Laws prescribe the Manner in which such Acts, Records and Proceedings shall be proved, and the Effect thereof.

Section 2 - State Citizens, Extradition

The Citizens of each State shall be entitled to all Privileges and Immunities of Citizens in the several States.

A Person charged in any State with Treason, Felony, or other Crime, who shall flee from Justice, and be found in another State, shall on demand of the executive Authority of the State from which he fled, be delivered up, to be removed to the State having Jurisdiction of the Crime.

(No Person held to Service or Labour in one State, under the Laws thereof, escaping into another, shall, in Consequence of any Law or Regulation therein, be discharged from such Service or Labour, But shall be delivered up on Claim of the Party to whom such Service or Labour may be due.) **(This clause in parentheses is superseded by the 13th Amendment.)**

Section 3 - New States

New States may be admitted by the Congress into this Union; but no new States shall be formed or erected within the Jurisdiction of any other State; nor any State be formed by the Junction of two or more States, or parts of States, without the Consent of the Legislatures of the States concerned as well as of the Congress.

The Congress shall have Power to dispose of and make all needful Rules and Regulations respecting the Territory or other Property belonging to the United States; and nothing in this Constitution shall be so construed as to Prejudice any Claims of the United States, or of any particular State.

Section 4 - Republican Government

The United States shall guarantee to every State in this Union a Republican Form of Government, and shall protect each of them against Invasion; and on Application of the Legislature, or of the Executive (when the Legislature cannot be convened) against domestic Violence.

Article V - Amendment

The Congress, whenever two thirds of both Houses shall deem it necessary, shall propose Amendments to this Constitution, or, on the Application of the Legislatures of two thirds of the several States, shall call a Convention for proposing Amendments, which, in either Case, shall be valid to all Intents and Purposes, as part of this Constitution, when ratified by the Legislatures of three fourths of the several States, or by Conventions in three fourths thereof, as the one or the other Mode of Ratification may be proposed by the Congress; Provided that no Amendment which may be made prior to the Year One thousand eight hundred and eight shall in any Manner affect the first and fourth Clauses in the Ninth Section of the first Article; and that no State, without its Consent, shall be deprived of its equal Suffrage in the Senate.

Article VI - Debts, Supremacy, Oaths

All Debts contracted and Engagements entered into, before the Adoption of this Constitution, shall be as valid against the United States under this Constitution, as under the Confederation.

This Constitution, and the Laws of the United States which shall be made in Pursuance thereof; and all Treaties made, or which shall be made, under the Authority of the United States, shall be the supreme Law of the Land; and the Judges in every State shall be bound thereby, any Thing in the Constitution or Laws of any State to the Contrary notwithstanding.

The Senators and Representatives before mentioned, and the Members of the several State Legislatures, and all executive and judicial Officers, both of the United States and of the several States, shall be bound by Oath or Affirmation, to support this Constitution; but no religious Test shall ever be required as a Qualification to any Office or public Trust under the United States.

Article VII - Ratification *Documents*

The Ratification of the Conventions of nine States, shall be sufficient for the Establishment of this Constitution between the States so ratifying the Same.

Done in Convention by the Unanimous Consent of the States present the Seventeenth Day of September in the Year of our Lord one thousand seven hundred and Eighty seven and of the Independence of the United States of America the Twelfth. In Witness whereof We have hereunto subscribed our Names.

Go Washington - President and deputy from Virginia

New Hampshire - John Langdon, Nicholas Gilman

Massachusetts - Nathaniel Gorham, Rufus King

Connecticut - Wm Saml Johnson, Roger Sherman

New York - Alexander Hamilton

New Jersey - Wil Livingston, David Brearley, Wm Paterson, Jona. Dayton

Pensylvania - B Franklin, Thomas Mifflin, Robt Morris, Geo. Clymer, Thos FitzSimons, Jared Ingersoll, James Wilson, Gouv Morris

Delaware - Geo. Read, Gunning Bedford jun, John Dickinson, Richard Bassett, Jaco. Broom

Maryland - James McHenry, Dan of St Tho Jenifer, Danl Carroll

Virginia - John Blair, James Madison Jr.

North Carolina - Wm Blount, Richd Dobbs Spaight, Hu Williamson

South Carolina - J. Rutledge, Charles Cotesworth Pinckney, Charles Pinckney, Pierce Butler

Georgia - William Few, Abr Baldwin

Attest: William Jackson, Secretary

The Amendments

The following are the Amendments to the Constitution. The first ten Amendments collectively are commonly known as the Bill of Rights.

Amendment 1 - Freedom of Religion, Press, Expression. Ratified 12/15/1791.

Congress shall make no law respecting an establishment of religion, or prohibiting the free exercise thereof; or abridging the freedom of speech, or of the press; or the right of the people peaceably to assemble, and to petition the Government for a redress of grievances.

Amendment 2 - Right to Bear Arms. Ratified 12/15/1791.

A well regulated Militia, being necessary to the security of a free State, the right of the people to keep and bear Arms, shall not be infringed.

Amendment 3 - Quartering of Soldiers. Ratified 12/15/1791.

No Soldier shall, in time of peace be quartered in any house, without the consent of the Owner, nor in time of war, but in a manner to be prescribed by law.

Amendment 4 - Search and Seizure. Ratified 12/15/1791.

The right of the people to be secure in their persons, houses, papers, and effects, against unreasonable searches and seizures, shall not be violated, and no Warrants shall issue, but upon probable cause, supported by Oath or affirmation, and particularly describing the place to be searched, and the persons or things to be seized.

Amendment 5 - Trial and Punishment, Compensation for Takings. Ratified 12/15/1791.

No person shall be held to answer for a capital, or otherwise infamous crime, unless on a presentment or indictment of a Grand Jury, except in cases arising in the land or naval forces, or in the Militia, when in actual service in time of War or public danger; nor shall any person be subject for the same offense to be twice put in jeopardy of life or limb; nor shall be compelled in any criminal case to be a witness against himself, nor be deprived of life, liberty, or property, without due process of law; nor shall private property be taken for public use, without just compensation.

Amendment 6 - Right to Speedy Trial, Confrontation of Witnesses. Ratified 12/15/1791.

In all criminal prosecutions, the accused shall enjoy the right to a speedy and public trial, by an impartial jury of the State and district wherein the crime shall have been committed, which district shall have been previously ascertained by law, and to be informed of the nature and cause of the accusation; to be confronted with the witnesses against him; to have compulsory process for obtaining witnesses in his favor, and to have the Assistance of Counsel for his defence.

Amendment 7 - Trial by Jury in Civil Cases. Ratified 12/15/1791.

In Suits at common law, where the value in controversy shall exceed twenty dollars, the right of trial by jury shall be preserved, and no fact tried by a jury, shall be otherwise re-examined in any Court of the United States, than according to the rules of the common law.

Amendment 8 - Cruel and Unusual Punishment. Ratified 12/15/1791.

Excessive bail shall not be required, nor excessive fines imposed, nor cruel and unusual punishments inflicted.

Amendment 9 - Construction of Constitution. Ratified 12/15/1791.

The enumeration in the Constitution, of certain rights, shall not be construed to deny or disparage others retained by the people.

Amendment 10 - Powers of the States and People. Ratified 12/15/1791.

The powers not delegated to the United States by the Constitution, nor prohibited by it to the States, are reserved to the States respectively, or to the people.

Amendment 11 - Judicial Limits. Ratified 2/7/1795.

The Judicial power of the United States shall not be construed to extend to any suit in law or equity, commenced or prosecuted against one of the

United States by Citizens of another State, or by Citizens or Subjects of any Foreign State.

Amendment 12 - Choosing the President, Vice-President. Ratified 6/15/1804.

The Electors shall meet in their respective states, and vote by ballot for President and Vice-President, one of whom, at least, shall not be an inhabitant of the same state with themselves; they shall name in their ballots the person voted for as President, and in distinct ballots the person voted for as Vice-President, and they shall make distinct lists of all persons voted for as President, and of all persons voted for as Vice-President and of the number of votes for each, which lists they shall sign and certify, and transmit sealed to the seat of the government of the United States, directed to the President of the Senate;

The President of the Senate shall, in the presence of the Senate and House of Representatives, open all the certificates and the votes shall then be counted;

The person having the greatest Number of votes for President, shall be the President, if such number be a majority of the whole number of Electors appointed; and if no person have such majority, then from the persons having the highest numbers not exceeding three on the list of those voted for as President, the House of Representatives shall choose immediately, by ballot, the President. But in choosing the President, the votes shall be taken by states, the representation from each state having one vote; a quorum for this purpose shall consist of a member or members from two-thirds of the states, and a majority of all the states shall be necessary to a choice. And if the House of Representatives shall not choose a President whenever the right of choice shall devolve upon them, before the fourth day of March next following, then the Vice-President shall act as President, as in the case of the death or other constitutional disability of the President.

The person having the greatest number of votes as Vice-President, shall be the Vice-President, if such number be a majority of the whole number of Electors appointed, and if no person have a majority, then from the two highest numbers on the list, the Senate shall choose the Vice-President; a quorum for the purpose shall consist of two-thirds of the whole number of

Senators, and a majority of the whole number shall be necessary to a choice. But no person constitutionally ineligible to the office of President shall be eligible to that of Vice-President of the United States.

Amendment 13 - Slavery Abolished. Ratified 12/6/1865.

1. Neither slavery nor involuntary servitude, except as a punishment for crime whereof the party shall have been duly convicted, shall exist within the United States, or any place subject to their jurisdiction.

2. Congress shall have power to enforce this article by appropriate legislation.

Amendment 14 - Citizenship Rights. Ratified 7/9/1868.

1. All persons born or naturalized in the United States, and subject to the jurisdiction thereof, are citizens of the United States and of the State wherein they reside. No State shall make or enforce any law which shall abridge the privileges or immunities of citizens of the United States; nor shall any State deprive any person of life, liberty, or property, without due process of law; nor deny to any person within its jurisdiction the equal protection of the laws.

2. Representatives shall be apportioned among the several States according to their respective numbers, counting the whole number of persons in each State, excluding Indians not taxed. But when the right to vote at any election for the choice of electors for President and Vice-President of the United States, Representatives in Congress, the Executive and Judicial officers of a State, or the members of the Legislature thereof, is denied to any of the male inhabitants of such State, being twenty-one years of age, and citizens of the United States, or in any way abridged, except for participation in rebellion, or other crime, the basis of representation therein shall be reduced in the proportion which the number of such male citizens shall bear to the whole number of male citizens twenty-one years of age in such State.

3. No person shall be a Senator or Representative in Congress, or elector of President and Vice-President, or hold any office, civil or military, under the United States, or under any State, who, having previously taken an oath, as a member of Congress, or as an officer of the United States, or as a member of any State legislature, or as an executive or judicial officer of any State, to

support the Constitution of the United States, shall have engaged in insurrection or rebellion against the same, or given aid or comfort to the enemies thereof. But Congress may by a vote of two-thirds of each House, remove such disability.

4. The validity of the public debt of the United States, authorized by law, including debts incurred for payment of pensions and bounties for services in suppressing insurrection or rebellion, shall not be questioned. But neither the United States nor any State shall assume or pay any debt or obligation incurred in aid of insurrection or rebellion against the United States, or any claim for the loss or emancipation of any slave; but all such debts, obligations and claims shall be held illegal and void.

5. The Congress shall have power to enforce, by appropriate legislation, the provisions of this article.

Amendment 15 - Race No Bar to Vote. Ratified 2/3/1870.

1. The right of citizens of the United States to vote shall not be denied or abridged by the United States or by any State on account of race, color, or previous condition of servitude.

2. The Congress shall have power to enforce this article by appropriate legislation.

Amendment 16 - Status of Income Tax Clarified. Ratified 2/3/1913.

The Congress shall have power to lay and collect taxes on incomes, from whatever source derived, without apportionment among the several States, and without regard to any census or enumeration.

Amendment 17 - Senators Elected by Popular Vote. Ratified 4/8/1913.

The Senate of the United States shall be composed of two Senators from each State, elected by the people thereof, for six years; and each Senator shall have one vote. The electors in each State shall have the qualifications requisite for electors of the most numerous branch of the State legislatures.

When vacancies happen in the representation of any State in the Senate, the executive authority of such State shall issue writs of election to fill such vacancies: Provided, That the legislature of any State may empower the executive thereof to make temporary appointments until the people fill the vacancies by election as the legislature may direct.

This amendment shall not be so construed as to affect the election or term of any Senator chosen before it becomes valid as part of the Constitution.

Amendment 18 - Liquor Abolished. Ratified 1/16/1919. Repealed by Amendment 21, 12/5/1933.

1. After one year from the ratification of this article the manufacture, sale, or transportation of intoxicating liquors within, the importation thereof into, or the exportation thereof from the United States and all territory subject to the jurisdiction thereof for beverage purposes is hereby prohibited.

2. The Congress and the several States shall have concurrent power to enforce this article by appropriate legislation.

3. This article shall be inoperative unless it shall have been ratified as an amendment to the Constitution by the legislatures of the several States, as provided in the Constitution, within seven years from the date of the submission hereof to the States by the Congress.

Amendment 19 - Women's Suffrage. Ratified 8/18/1920.

The right of citizens of the United States to vote shall not be denied or abridged by the United States or by any State on account of sex.

Congress shall have power to enforce this article by appropriate legislation.

Amendment 20 - Presidential, Congressional Terms. Ratified 1/23/1933.

1. The terms of the President and Vice President shall end at noon on the 20th day of January, and the terms of Senators and Representatives at noon on the 3d day of January, of the years in which such terms would have ended if this article had not been ratified; and the terms of their successors shall then begin.

2. The Congress shall assemble at least once in every year, and such meeting shall begin at noon on the 3d day of January, unless they shall by law appoint a different day.

3. If, at the time fixed for the beginning of the term of the President, the President elect shall have died, the Vice President elect shall become President. If a President shall not have been chosen before the time fixed for the beginning of his term, or if the President elect shall have failed to qualify, then the Vice President elect shall act as President until a President shall have qualified; and the Congress may by law provide for the case wherein neither a President elect nor a Vice President elect shall have qualified, declaring who shall then act as President, or the manner in which one who is to act shall be selected, and such person shall act accordingly until a President or Vice President shall have qualified.

4. The Congress may by law provide for the case of the death of any of the persons from whom the House of Representatives may choose a President whenever the right of choice shall have devolved upon them, and for the case of the death of any of the persons from whom the Senate may choose a Vice President whenever the right of choice shall have devolved upon them.

5. Sections 1 and 2 shall take effect on the 15th day of October following the ratification of this article.

6. This article shall be inoperative unless it shall have been ratified as an amendment to the Constitution by the legislatures of three-fourths of the several States within seven years from the date of its submission.

Amendment 21 - Amendment 18 Repealed. Ratified 12/5/1933.

1. The eighteenth article of amendment to the Constitution of the United States is hereby repealed.

2. The transportation or importation into any State, Territory, or possession of the United States for delivery or use therein of intoxicating liquors, in violation of the laws thereof, is hereby prohibited.

3. The article shall be inoperative unless it shall have been ratified as an amendment to the Constitution by conventions in the several States, as provided in the Constitution, within seven years from the date of the submission hereof to the States by the Congress.

Amendment 22 - Presidential Term Limits. Ratified 2/27/1951.

1. No person shall be elected to the office of the President more than twice, and no person who has held the office of President, or acted as President, for more than two years of a term to which some other person was elected President shall be elected to the office of the President more than once. But this Article shall not apply to any person holding the office of President, when this Article was proposed by the Congress, and shall not prevent any person who may be holding the office of President, or acting as President, during the term within which this Article becomes operative from holding the office of President or acting as President during the remainder of such term.

2. This article shall be inoperative unless it shall have been ratified as an amendment to the Constitution by the legislatures of three-fourths of the several States within seven years from the date of its submission to the States by the Congress.

Amendment 23 - Presidential Vote for District of Columbia. Ratified 3/29/1961.

1. The District constituting the seat of Government of the United States shall appoint in such manner as the Congress may direct: A number of electors of President and Vice President equal to the whole number of Senators and Representatives in Congress to which the District would be entitled if it were a State, but in no event more than the least populous State; they shall be in addition to those appointed by the States, but they shall be considered, for the purposes of the election of President and Vice President, to be electors appointed by a State; and they shall meet in the District and perform such duties as provided by the twelfth article of amendment.

2. The Congress shall have power to enforce this article by appropriate legislation.

Amendment 24 - Poll Tax Barred. Ratified 1/23/1964.

1. The right of citizens of the United States to vote in any primary or other election for President or Vice President, for electors for President or Vice President, or for Senator or Representative in Congress, shall not be denied or abridged by the United States or any State by reason of failure to pay any poll tax or other tax.

2. The Congress shall have power to enforce this article by appropriate legislation.

Amendment 25 - Presidential Disability and Succession. Ratified 2/10/1967.

1. In case of the removal of the President from office or of his death or resignation, the Vice President shall become President.

2. Whenever there is a vacancy in the office of the Vice President, the President shall nominate a Vice President who shall take office upon confirmation by a majority vote of both Houses of Congress.

3. Whenever the President transmits to the President pro tempore of the Senate and the Speaker of the House of Representatives his written declaration that he is unable to discharge the powers and duties of his office, and until he transmits to them a written declaration to the contrary, such powers and duties shall be discharged by the Vice President as Acting President.

4. Whenever the Vice President and a majority of either the principal officers of the executive departments or of such other body as Congress may by law provide, transmit to the President pro tempore of the Senate and the Speaker of the House of Representatives their written declaration that the President is unable to discharge the powers and duties of his office, the Vice President shall immediately assume the powers and duties of the office as Acting President.

Thereafter, when the President transmits to the President pro tempore of the Senate and the Speaker of the House of Representatives his written declaration that no inability exists, he shall resume the powers and duties of his office unless the Vice President and a majority of either the principal officers of the executive department or of such other body as Congress may by law provide, transmit within four days to the President pro tempore of the Senate and the Speaker of the House of Representatives their written declaration that the President is unable to discharge the powers and duties of his office. Thereupon Congress shall decide the issue, assembling within forty eight hours for that purpose if not in session. If the Congress, within twenty one days after receipt of the latter written declaration, or, if Congress is not in session, within twenty one days after Congress is required to assemble, determines by two thirds vote of both Houses that the President is unable to discharge the powers and duties of his office, the Vice President shall continue to discharge the same as Acting President; otherwise, the President shall resume the powers and duties of his office.

Amendment 26 - Voting Age Set to 18 Years. Ratified 7/1/1971.

1. The right of citizens of the United States, who are eighteen years of age or older, to vote shall not be denied or abridged by the United States or by any State on account of age.

2. The Congress shall have power to enforce this article by appropriate legislation.

Amendment 27 - Limiting Congressional Pay Increases. Ratified 5/7/1992.

No law, varying the compensation for the services of the Senators and Representatives, shall take effect, until an election of Representatives shall have intervened.

Appendix 2 – President Washington's farewell address 1776

Friends and Citizens:

The period for a new election of a citizen to administer the executive government of the United States being not far distant, and the time actually arrived when your thoughts must be employed in designating the person who is to be clothed with that important trust, it appears to me proper, especially as it may conduce to a more distinct expression of the public voice, that I should now apprise you of the resolution I have formed, to decline being considered among the number of those out of whom a choice is to be made.

I beg you, at the same time, to do me the justice to be assured that this resolution has not been taken without a strict regard to all the considerations appertaining to the relation which binds a dutiful citizen to his country; and that in withdrawing the tender of service, which silence in my situation might imply, I am influenced by no diminution of zeal for your future interest, no deficiency of grateful respect for your past kindness, but am supported by a full conviction that the step is compatible with both.

The acceptance of, and continuance hitherto in, the office to which your suffrages have twice called me have been a uniform sacrifice of inclination to the opinion of duty and to a deference for what appeared to be your desire. I constantly hoped that it would have been much earlier in my power, consistently with motives which I was not at liberty to disregard, to return to that retirement from which I had been reluctantly drawn. The strength of my inclination to do this, previous to the last election, had even led to the preparation of an address to declare it to you; but mature reflection on the then perplexed and critical posture of our affairs with foreign nations, and the unanimous advice of persons entitled to my confidence, impelled me to abandon the idea.

I rejoice that the state of your concerns, external as well as internal, no longer renders the pursuit of inclination incompatible with the sentiment of duty or propriety, and am persuaded, whatever partiality may be retained for my services, that, in the present circumstances of our country, you will not disapprove my determination to retire.

The impressions with which I first undertook the arduous trust were explained on the proper occasion. In the discharge of this trust, I will only say that I have, with good intentions, contributed towards the organization and administration of the government the best exertions of which a very fallible judgment was capable. Not unconscious in the outset of the inferiority of my qualifications, experience in my own eyes, perhaps still more in the eyes of others, has strengthened the motives to diffidence of myself; and every day the increasing weight of years admonishes me more and more that the shade of retirement is as necessary to me as it will be welcome. Satisfied that if any circumstances have given peculiar value to my services, they were temporary, I have the consolation to believe that, while choice and prudence invite me to quit the political scene, patriotism does not forbid it.

In looking forward to the moment which is intended to terminate the career of my public life, my feelings do not permit me to suspend the deep acknowledgment of that debt of gratitude which I owe to my beloved country for the many honors it has conferred upon me; still more for the steadfast confidence with which it has supported me; and for the opportunities I have thence enjoyed of manifesting my inviolable attachment, by services faithful and persevering, though in usefulness unequal to my zeal. If benefits have resulted to our country from these services, let it always be remembered to your praise, and as an instructive example in our annals, that under circumstances in which the passions, agitated in every direction, were liable to mislead, amidst appearances sometimes dubious, vicissitudes of fortune often discouraging, in situations in which not unfrequently want of success has countenanced the spirit of criticism, the constancy of your support was the essential prop of the efforts, and a guarantee of the plans by which they were effected. Profoundly penetrated with this idea, I shall carry it with me to my grave, as a strong incitement to unceasing vows that heaven may continue to you the choicest tokens of its beneficence; that your union and brotherly affection may be perpetual; that the free Constitution, which is the work of your hands, may be sacredly maintained; that its administration in every department may be stamped with wisdom and virtue; that, in fine, the happiness of the people of these States, under the auspices of liberty, may be made complete by so careful a preservation and so prudent a use of this blessing as will acquire to them the glory of recommending it to the applause, the affection, and adoption of every nation which is yet a stranger to it.

Here, perhaps, I ought to stop. But a solicitude for your welfare, which cannot end but with my life, and the apprehension of danger, natural to that solicitude, urge me, on an occasion like the present, to offer to your solemn contemplation, and to recommend to your frequent review, some sentiments which are the result of much reflection, of no inconsiderable observation, and which appear to me all-important to the permanency of your felicity as a people. These will be offered to you with the more freedom, as you can only see in them the disinterested warnings of a parting friend, who can possibly have no personal motive to bias his counsel. Nor can I forget, as an encouragement to it, your indulgent reception of my sentiments on a former and not dissimilar occasion.

Interwoven as is the love of liberty with every ligament of your hearts, no recommendation of mine is necessary to fortify or confirm the attachment.

The unity of government which constitutes you one people is also now dear to you. It is justly so, for it is a main pillar in the edifice of your real independence, the support of your tranquility at home, your peace abroad; of your safety; of your prosperity; of that very liberty which you so highly prize. But as it is easy to foresee that, from different causes and from different quarters, much pains will be taken, many artifices employed to weaken in your minds the conviction of this truth; as this is the point in your political fortress against which the batteries of internal and external enemies will be most constantly and actively (though often covertly and insidiously) directed, it is of infinite moment that you should properly estimate the immense value of your national union to your collective and individual happiness; that you should cherish a cordial, habitual, and immovable attachment to it; accustoming yourselves to think and speak of it as of the palladium of your political safety and prosperity; watching for its preservation with jealous anxiety; discountenancing whatever may suggest even a suspicion that it can in any event be abandoned; and indignantly frowning upon the first dawning of every attempt to alienate any portion of our country from the rest, or to enfeeble the sacred ties which now link together the various parts.

For this you have every inducement of sympathy and interest. Citizens, by birth or choice, of a common country, that country has a right to concentrate your affections. The name of American, which belongs to you in your national capacity, must always exalt the just pride of patriotism more than any appellation derived from local discriminations. With slight shades of difference, you have the same religion, manners, habits, and political principles. You have in a common cause fought and triumphed together; the independence and liberty you possess are the work of joint counsels, and joint efforts of common dangers, sufferings, and successes.

But these considerations, however powerfully they address themselves to your sensibility, are greatly outweighed by those which apply more immediately to your interest. Here every portion of our country finds the most commanding motives for carefully guarding and preserving the union of the whole.

The North, in an unrestrained intercourse with the South, protected by the equal laws of a common government, finds in the productions of the latter great additional resources of maritime and commercial enterprise and precious materials of manufacturing industry. The South, in the same intercourse, benefiting by the agency of the North, sees its agriculture grow and its commerce expand. Turning partly into its own channels the seamen of the North, it finds its particular navigation invigorated; and, while it contributes, in different ways, to nourish and increase the general mass of the national navigation, it looks forward to the protection of a maritime strength, to which itself is unequally adapted. The East, in a like intercourse with the West, already finds, and in the progressive improvement of interior communications by land and water, will more and more find a valuable vent for the commodities which it brings from abroad, or manufactures at home. The West derives from the East supplies requisite to its growth and comfort, and, what is perhaps of still greater consequence, it must of necessity owe the secure enjoyment of indispensable outlets for its own productions to the weight, influence, and the future maritime strength of the Atlantic side of the Union, directed by an indissoluble community of interest as one nation. Any other tenure by which the West can hold this essential advantage, whether derived from its own separate strength, or from an apostate and unnatural connection with any foreign power, must be intrinsically precarious.

While, then, every part of our country thus feels an immediate and particular interest in union, all the parts combined cannot fail to find in the united mass of means and efforts greater strength, greater resource, proportionably greater security from external danger, a less frequent interruption of their peace by foreign nations; and, what is of inestimable value, they must derive from union an exemption from those broils and wars between themselves, which so frequently afflict neighboring countries not tied together by the same governments, which their own rival ships alone would be sufficient to produce, but which opposite foreign alliances, attachments, and intrigues would stimulate and embitter. Hence, likewise, they will avoid the necessity of those overgrown military establishments which, under any form of government, are inauspicious to liberty, and which are to be regarded as particularly hostile to republican liberty. In this sense it is that your union ought to be considered as a main prop of your liberty, and that the love of the one ought to endear to you the preservation of the other.

These considerations speak a persuasive language to every reflecting and virtuous mind, and exhibit the continuance of the Union as a primary object of patriotic desire. Is there a doubt whether a common government can embrace so large a sphere? Let experience solve it. To listen to mere speculation in such a case were criminal. We are authorized to hope that a proper organization of the whole with the auxiliary agency of governments for the respective subdivisions, will afford a happy issue to the experiment. It is well worth a fair and full experiment. With such powerful and obvious motives to union, affecting all parts of our country, while experience shall not have demonstrated its impracticability, there will always be reason to distrust the patriotism of those who in any quarter may endeavor to weaken its bands.

In contemplating the causes which may disturb our Union, it occurs as matter of serious concern that any ground should have been furnished for characterizing parties by geographical discriminations, Northern and Southern, Atlantic and Western; whence designing men may endeavor to excite a belief that there is a real difference of local interests and views. One of the expedients of party to acquire influence within particular districts is to misrepresent the opinions and aims of other districts. You cannot shield yourselves too much against the jealousies and heartburnings which spring from these misrepresentations; they tend to render alien to each other those who ought to be bound together by fraternal affection. The inhabitants of our Western country have lately had a useful lesson on this head; they have seen, in the negotiation by the Executive, and in the unanimous ratification by the Senate, of the treaty with Spain, and in the universal satisfaction at that event, throughout the United States, a decisive proof how unfounded were the suspicions propagated among them of a policy in the General Government and in the Atlantic States unfriendly to their interests in regard to the Mississippi; they have been witnesses to the formation of two treaties, that with Great Britain, and that with Spain, which secure to them everything they could desire, in respect to our foreign relations, towards confirming their prosperity. Will it not be their wisdom to rely for the preservation of these advantages on the Union by which they were procured ? Will they not henceforth be deaf to those advisers, if such there are, who would sever them from their brethren and connect them with aliens?

To the efficacy and permanency of your Union, a government for the whole is indispensable. No alliance, however strict, between the parts can be an adequate substitute; they must inevitably experience the infractions and interruptions which all alliances in all times have experienced. Sensible of this momentous truth, you have improved upon your first essay, by the adoption of a constitution of government better calculated than your former for an intimate union, and for the efficacious management of your common concerns. This government, the offspring of our own choice, uninfluenced and unawed, adopted upon full investigation and mature deliberation, completely free in its principles, in the distribution of its powers, uniting security with energy, and containing within itself a provision for its own amendment, has a just claim to your confidence and your support. Respect for its authority, compliance with its laws, acquiescence in its measures, are duties enjoined by the fundamental maxims of true liberty. The basis of our political systems is the right of the people to make and to alter their constitutions of government. But the Constitution which at any time exists, till changed by an explicit and authentic act of the whole people, is sacredly obligatory upon all. The very idea of the power and the right of the people to establish government presupposes the duty of every individual to obey the established government.

All obstructions to the execution of the laws, all combinations and associations, under whatever plausible character, with the real design to direct, control, counteract, or awe the regular deliberation and action of the constituted authorities, are destructive of this fundamental principle, and of fatal tendency. They serve to organize faction, to give it an artificial and extraordinary force; to put, in the place of the delegated will of the nation the will of a party, often a small but artful and enterprising minority of the community; and, according to the alternate triumphs of different parties, to make the public administration the mirror of the ill-concerted and incongruous projects of faction, rather than the organ of consistent and wholesome plans digested by common counsels and modified by mutual interests.

However combinations or associations of the above description may now and then answer popular ends, they are likely, in the course of time and things, to become potent engines, by which cunning, ambitious, and unprincipled men will be enabled to subvert the power of the people and to usurp for themselves the reins of government, destroying afterwards the very engines which have lifted them to unjust dominion.

Towards the preservation of your government, and the permanency of your present happy state, it is requisite, not only that you steadily discountenance irregular oppositions to its acknowledged authority, but also that you resist with care the spirit of innovation upon its principles, however specious the pretexts. One method of assault may be to effect, in the forms of the Constitution, alterations which will impair the energy of the system, and thus to undermine what cannot be directly overthrown. In all the changes to which you may be invited, remember that time and habit are at least as necessary to fix the true character of governments as of other human institutions; that experience is the surest standard by which to test the real tendency of the existing constitution of a country; that facility in changes, upon the credit of mere hypothesis and opinion, exposes to perpetual change, from the endless variety of hypothesis and opinion; and remember, especially, that for the efficient management of your common interests, in a country so extensive as ours, a government of as much vigor as is consistent with the perfect security of liberty is indispensable. Liberty itself will find in such a government, with powers properly distributed and adjusted, its surest guardian. It is, indeed, little else than a name, where the government is too feeble to withstand the enterprises of faction, to confine each member of the society within the limits prescribed by the laws, and to maintain all in the secure and tranquil enjoyment of the rights of person and property.

I have already intimated to you the danger of parties in the State, with particular reference to the founding of them on geographical discriminations. Let me now take a more comprehensive view, and warn you in the most solemn manner against the baneful effects of the spirit of party generally.

This spirit, unfortunately, is inseparable from our nature, having its root in the strongest passions of the human mind. It exists under different shapes in all governments, more or less stifled, controlled, or repressed; but, in those of the popular form, it is seen in its greatest rankness, and is truly their worst enemy.

The alternate domination of one faction over another, sharpened by the spirit of revenge, natural to party dissension, which in different ages and countries has perpetrated the most horrid enormities, is itself a frightful despotism. But this leads at length to a more formal and permanent despotism. The disorders and miseries which result gradually incline the minds of men to seek security and repose in the absolute power of an individual; and sooner or later the chief of some prevailing faction, more able or more fortunate than his competitors, turns this disposition to the purposes of his own elevation, on the ruins of public liberty.

Without looking forward to an extremity of this kind (which nevertheless ought not to be entirely out of sight), the common and continual mischiefs of the spirit of party are sufficient to make it the interest and duty of a wise people to discourage and restrain it.

It serves always to distract the public councils and enfeeble the public administration. It agitates the community with ill-founded jealousies and false alarms, kindles the animosity of one part against another, foments occasionally riot and insurrection. It opens the door to foreign influence and corruption, which finds a facilitated access to the government itself through the channels of party passions. Thus the policy and the will of one country are subjected to the policy and will of another.

There is an opinion that parties in free countries are useful checks upon the administration of the government and serve to keep alive the spirit of liberty. This within certain limits is probably true; and in governments of a monarchical cast, patriotism may look with indulgence, if not with favor, upon the spirit of party. But in those of the popular character, in governments purely elective, it is a spirit not to be encouraged. From their natural tendency, it is certain there will always be enough of that spirit for every salutary purpose. And there being constant danger of excess, the effort ought to be by force of public opinion, to mitigate and assuage it. A fire not to be quenched, it demands a uniform vigilance to prevent its bursting into a flame, lest, instead of warming, it should consume.

It is important, likewise, that the habits of thinking in a free country should inspire caution in those entrusted with its administration, to confine themselves within their respective constitutional spheres, avoiding in the exercise of the powers of one department to encroach upon another. The spirit of encroachment tends to consolidate the powers of all the departments in one, and thus to create, whatever the form of government, a real despotism. A just estimate of that love of power, and proneness to abuse it, which predominates in the human heart, is sufficient to satisfy us of the truth of this position. The necessity of reciprocal checks in the exercise of political power, by dividing and distributing it into different depositaries, and constituting each the guardian of the public weal against invasions by the others, has been evinced by experiments ancient and modern; some of them in our country and under our own eyes. To preserve them must be as necessary as to institute them. If, in the opinion of the people, the distribution or modification of the constitutional powers be in any particular wrong, let it be corrected by an amendment in the way which the Constitution designates. But let there be no change by usurpation; for though this, in one instance, may be the instrument of good, it is the customary weapon by which free governments are destroyed. The precedent must always greatly overbalance in permanent evil any partial or transient benefit, which the use can at any time yield.

Of all the dispositions and habits which lead to political prosperity, religion and morality are indispensable supports. In vain would that man claim the tribute of patriotism, who should labor to subvert these great pillars of human happiness, these firmest props of the duties of men and citizens. The mere politician, equally with the pious man, ought to respect and to cherish them. A volume could not trace all their connections with private and public felicity. Let it simply be asked: Where is the security for property, for reputation, for life, if the sense of religious obligation desert the oaths which are the instruments of investigation in courts of justice ? And let us with caution indulge the supposition that morality can be maintained without religion. Whatever may be conceded to the influence of refined education on minds of peculiar structure, reason and experience both forbid us to expect that national morality can prevail in exclusion of religious principle.

It is substantially true that virtue or morality is a necessary spring of popular government. The rule, indeed, extends with more or less force to every species of free government. Who that is a sincere friend to it can look with indifference upon attempts to shake the foundation of the fabric?

Promote then, as an object of primary importance, institutions for the general diffusion of knowledge. In proportion as the structure of a government gives force to public opinion, it is essential that public opinion should be enlightened.

As a very important source of strength and security, cherish public credit. One method of preserving it is to use it as sparingly as possible, avoiding occasions of expense by cultivating peace, but remembering also that timely disbursements to prepare for danger frequently prevent much greater disbursements to repel it, avoiding likewise the accumulation of debt, not only by shunning occasions of expense, but by vigorous exertion in time of peace to discharge the debts which unavoidable wars may have occasioned, not ungenerously throwing upon posterity the burden which we ourselves ought to bear. The execution of these maxims belongs to your representatives, but it is necessary that public opinion should co-operate. To facilitate to them the performance of their duty, it is essential that you should practically bear in mind that towards the payment of debts there must be revenue; that to have revenue there must be taxes; that no taxes can be devised which are not more or less inconvenient and unpleasant; that the intrinsic embarrassment, inseparable from the selection of the proper objects (which is always a choice of difficulties), ought to be a decisive motive for a candid construction of the conduct of the government in making it, and for a spirit of acquiescence in the measures for obtaining revenue, which the public exigencies may at any time dictate.

Observe good faith and justice towards all nations; cultivate peace and harmony with all. Religion and morality enjoin this conduct; and can it be, that good policy does not equally enjoin it - It will be worthy of a free, enlightened, and at no distant period, a great nation, to give to mankind the magnanimous and too novel example of a people always guided by an exalted justice and benevolence. Who can doubt that, in the course of time and things, the fruits of such a plan would richly repay any temporary advantages which might be lost by a steady adherence to it ? Can it be that Providence has not connected the permanent felicity of a nation with its virtue ? The experiment, at least, is recommended by every sentiment which ennobles human nature. Alas! is it rendered impossible by its vices?

In the execution of such a plan, nothing is more essential than that permanent, inveterate antipathies against particular nations, and passionate attachments for others, should be excluded; and that, in place of them, just and amicable feelings towards all should be cultivated. The nation which indulges towards another a habitual hatred or a habitual fondness is in some degree a slave. It is a slave to its animosity or to its affection, either of which is sufficient to lead it astray from its duty and its interest. Antipathy in one nation against another disposes each more readily to offer insult and injury, to lay hold of slight causes of umbrage, and to be haughty and intractable, when accidental or trifling occasions of dispute occur. Hence, frequent collisions, obstinate, envenomed, and bloody contests. The nation, prompted by ill-will and resentment, sometimes impels to war the government, contrary to the best calculations of policy. The government sometimes participates in the national propensity, and adopts through passion what reason would reject; at other times it makes the animosity of the nation subservient to projects of hostility instigated by pride, ambition, and other sinister and pernicious motives. The peace often, sometimes perhaps the liberty, of nations, has been the victim.

So likewise, a passionate attachment of one nation for another produces a variety of evils. Sympathy for the favorite nation, facilitating the illusion of an imaginary common interest in cases where no real common interest exists, and infusing into one the enmities of the other, betrays the former into a participation in the quarrels and wars of the latter without adequate inducement or justification. It leads also to concessions to the favorite nation of privileges denied to others which is apt doubly to injure the nation making the concessions; by unnecessarily parting with what ought to have been retained, and by exciting jealousy, ill-will, and a disposition to retaliate, in the parties from whom equal privileges are withheld. And it gives to ambitious, corrupted, or deluded citizens (who devote themselves to the favorite nation), facility to betray or sacrifice the interests of their own country, without odium, sometimes even with popularity; gilding, with the appearances of a virtuous sense of obligation, a commendable deference for public opinion, or a laudable zeal for public good, the base or foolish compliances of ambition, corruption, or infatuation.

As avenues to foreign influence in innumerable ways, such attachments are particularly alarming to the truly enlightened and independent patriot. How many opportunities do they afford to tamper with domestic factions, to practice the arts of seduction, to mislead public opinion, to influence or awe the public councils. Such an attachment of a small or weak towards a great and powerful nation dooms the former to be the satellite of the latter.

Against the insidious wiles of foreign influence (I conjure you to believe me, fellow-citizens) the jealousy of a free people ought to be constantly awake, since history and experience prove that foreign influence is one of the most baneful foes of republican government. But that jealousy to be useful must be impartial; else it becomes the instrument of the very influence to be avoided, instead of a defense against it. Excessive partiality for one foreign nation and excessive dislike of another cause those whom they actuate to see danger only on one side, and serve to veil and even second the arts of influence on the other. Real patriots who may resist the intrigues of the favorite are liable to become suspected and odious, while its tools and dupes usurp the applause and confidence of the people, to surrender their interests.

The great rule of conduct for us in regard to foreign nations is in extending our commercial relations, to have with them as little political connection as possible. So far as we have already formed engagements, let them be fulfilled with perfect good faith. Here let us stop. Europe has a set of primary interests which to us have none; or a very remote relation. Hence she must be engaged in frequent controversies, the causes of which are essentially foreign to our concerns. Hence, therefore, it must be unwise in us to implicate ourselves by artificial ties in the ordinary vicissitudes of her politics, or the ordinary combinations and collisions of her friendships or enmities.

Our detached and distant situation invites and enables us to pursue a different course. If we remain one people under an efficient government. the period is not far off when we may defy material injury from external annoyance; when we may take such an attitude as will cause the neutrality we may at any time resolve upon to be scrupulously respected; when belligerent nations, under the impossibility of making acquisitions upon us, will not lightly hazard the giving us provocation; when we may choose peace or war, as our interest, guided by justice, shall counsel.

Why forego the advantages of so peculiar a situation? Why quit our own to stand upon foreign ground? Why, by interweaving our destiny with that of any part of Europe, entangle our peace and prosperity in the toils of European ambition, rivalship, interest, humor or caprice?

It is our true policy to steer clear of permanent alliances with any portion of the foreign world; so far, I mean, as we are now at liberty to do it; for let me not be understood as capable of patronizing infidelity to existing engagements. I hold the maxim no less applicable to public than to private affairs, that honesty is always the best policy. I repeat it, therefore, let those engagements be observed in their genuine sense. But, in my opinion, it is unnecessary and would be unwise to extend them.

Taking care always to keep ourselves by suitable establishments on a respectable defensive posture, we may safely trust to temporary alliances for extraordinary emergencies.

Harmony, liberal intercourse with all nations, are recommended by policy, humanity, and interest. But even our commercial policy should hold an equal and impartial hand; neither seeking nor granting exclusive favors or preferences; consulting the natural course of things; diffusing and diversifying by gentle means the streams of commerce, but forcing nothing; establishing (with powers so disposed, in order to give trade a stable course, to define the rights of our merchants, and to enable the government to support them) conventional rules of intercourse, the best that present circumstances and mutual opinion will permit, but temporary, and liable to be from time to time abandoned or varied, as experience and circumstances shall dictate; constantly keeping in view that it is folly in one nation to look for disinterested favors from another; that it must pay with a portion of its independence for whatever it may accept under that character; that, by such acceptance, it may place itself in the condition of having given equivalents for nominal favors, and yet of being reproached with ingratitude for not giving more. There can be no greater error than to expect or calculate upon real favors from nation to nation. It is an illusion, which experience must cure, which a just pride ought to discard.

In offering to you, my countrymen, these counsels of an old and affectionate friend, I dare not hope they will make the strong and lasting impression I could wish; that they will control the usual current of the passions, or prevent our nation from running the course which has hitherto marked the destiny of nations. But, if I may even flatter myself that they may be productive of some partial benefit, some occasional good; that they may now and then recur to moderate the fury of party spirit, to warn against the mischiefs of foreign intrigue, to guard against the impostures of pretended patriotism; this hope will be a full recompense for the solicitude for your welfare, by which they have been dictated.

How far in the discharge of my official duties I have been guided by the principles which have been delineated, the public records and other evidences of my conduct must witness to you and to the world. To myself, the assurance of my own conscience is, that I have at least believed myself to be guided by them.

In relation to the still subsisting war in Europe, my proclamation of the twenty-second of April, 1793, is the index of my plan. Sanctioned by your approving voice, and by that of your representatives in both houses of Congress, the spirit of that measure has continually governed me, uninfluenced by any attempts to deter or divert me from it.

After deliberate examination, with the aid of the best lights I could obtain, I was well satisfied that our country, under all the circumstances of the case, had a right to take, and was bound in duty and interest to take, a neutral position. Having taken it, I determined, as far as should depend upon me, to maintain it, with moderation, perseverance, and firmness.

The considerations which respect the right to hold this conduct, it is not necessary on this occasion to detail. I will only observe that, according to my understanding of the matter, that right, so far from being denied by any of the belligerent powers, has been virtually admitted by all.

The duty of holding a neutral conduct may be inferred, without anything more, from the obligation which justice and humanity impose on every nation, in cases in which it is free to act, to maintain inviolate the relations of peace and amity towards other nations.

The inducements of interest for observing that conduct will best be referred to your own reflections and experience. With me a predominant motive has been to endeavor to gain time to our country to settle and mature its yet recent institutions, and to progress without interruption to that degree of strength and consistency which is necessary to give it, humanly speaking, the command of its own fortunes.

Though, in reviewing the incidents of my administration, I am unconscious of intentional error, I am nevertheless too sensible of my defects not to think it probable that I may have committed many errors. Whatever they may be, I fervently beseech the Almighty to avert or mitigate the evils to which they may tend. I shall also carry with me the hope that my country will never cease to view them with indulgence; and that, after forty five years of my life dedicated to its service with an upright zeal, the faults of incompetent abilities will be consigned to oblivion, as myself must soon be to the mansions of rest.

Relying on its kindness in this as in other things, and actuated by that fervent love towards it, which is so natural to a man who views in it the native soil of himself and his progenitors for several generations, I anticipate with pleasing expectation that retreat in which I promise myself to realize, without alloy, the sweet enjoyment of partaking, in the midst of my fellow-citizens, the benign influence of good laws under a free government, the ever-favorite object of my heart, and the happy reward, as I trust, of our mutual cares, labors, and dangers.

Charles F. Stamper

Appendix 3 – President Jefferson's letter to Samuel Kercheval

SIR, -- I duly received your favor of June the 13th, with the copy of the letters on the calling a convention, on which you are pleased to ask my opinion. I have not been in the habit of mysterious reserve on any subject, nor of buttoning up my opinions within my own doublet. On the contrary, while in public service especially, I thought the public entitled to frankness, and intimately to know whom they employed. But I am now retired: I resign myself, as a passenger, with confidence to those at present at the helm, and ask but for rest, peace and good will. The question you propose, on equal representation, has become a party one, in which I wish to take no public share. Yet, if it be asked for your own satisfaction only, and not to be quoted before the public, I have no motive to withhold it, and the less from you, as it coincides with your own. At the birth of our republic, I committed that opinion to the world, in the draught of a constitution annexed to the "Notes on Virginia," in which a provision was inserted for a representation permanently equal. The infancy of the subject at that moment, and our inexperience of self-government, occasioned gross departures in that draught from genuine republican canons. In truth, the abuses of monarchy had so much filled all the space of political contemplation, that we imagined everything republican which was not monarchy. We had not yet penetrated to the mother principle, that "governments are republican only in proportion as they embody the will of their people, and execute it." Hence, our first constitutions had really no leading principles in them. But experience and reflection have but more and more confirmed me in the particular importance of the equal representation then proposed. On that point, then, I am entirely in sentiment with your letters; and only lament that a copy--right of your pamphlet prevents their appearance in the newspapers, where alone they would be generally read, and produce general effect. The present vacancy too, of other matter, would give them place in every paper, and bring the question home to every man's conscience.

But inequality of representation in both Houses of our legislature, is not the only republican heresy in this first essay of our revolutionary patriots at forming a constitution. For let it be agreed that a government is republican in proportion as every member composing it has his equal voice in the direction of its concerns (not indeed in person, which would be impracticable beyond the limits of a city, or small township, but) by representatives chosen by himself, and responsible to him at short periods, and let us bring to the test of this canon every branch of our constitution.

In the legislature, the House of Representatives is chosen by less than half the people, and not at all in proportion to those who do choose. The Senate are still more disproportionate, and for long terms of irresponsibility. In the Executive, the Governor is entirely independent of the choice of the people, and of their control; his Council equally so, and at best but a fifth wheel to a wagon. In the Judiciary, the judges of the highest courts are dependent on none but themselves. In England, where judges were named and removable at the will of an hereditary executive, from which branch most misrule was feared, and has flowed, it was a great point gained, by fixing them for life, to make them independent of that executive. But in a government founded on the public will, this principle operates in an opposite direction, and against that will. There, too, they were still removable on a concurrence of the executive and legislative branches. But we have made them independent of the nation itself. They are irremovable, but by their own body, for any depravities of conduct, and even by their own body for the imbecilities of dotage. The justices of the inferior courts are self-chosen, are for life, and perpetuate their own body in succession forever, so that a faction once possessing themselves of the bench of a county, can never be broken up, but hold their county in chains, forever indissoluble. Yet these justices are the real executive as well as judiciary, in all our minor and most ordinary concerns. They tax us at will; fill the office of sheriff, the most important of all the executive officers of the county; name nearly all our military leaders, which leaders, once named, are removable but by themselves. The juries, our judges of all fact, and of law when they choose it, are not selected by the people, nor amenable to them. They are chosen by an officer named by the court and executive. Chosen, did I say? Picked up by the sheriff from the loungings of the court yard, after everything respectable has retired from it. Where then is our republicanism to be found? Not in our constitution certainly, but merely in the spirit of our people. That would oblige even a despot to govern us republicanly. Owing to this spirit, and to nothing in the form of our constitution, all things have gone well. But this fact, so triumphantly misquoted by the enemies of reformation, is not the fruit of our constitution, but has prevailed in spite of it. Our functionaries have done well, because generally honest men. If any were not so, they feared to show it.

But it will be said, it is easier to find faults than to amend them. I do not think their amendment so difficult as is pretended. Only lay down true principles, and adhere to them inflexibly. Do not be frightened into their surrender by the alarms of the timid, or the croakings of wealth against the ascendency of the people. If experience be called for, appeal to that of our fifteen or twenty governments for forty years, and show me where the people have done half the mischief in these forty years, that a single despot would have done in a single year; or show half the riots and rebellions, the crimes and the punishments, which have taken place in any single nation, under kingly government, during the same period. The true foundation of republican government is the equal right of every citizen, in his person and property, and in their management. Try by this, as a tally, every provision of our constitution, and see if it hangs directly on the will of the people. Reduce your legislature to a convenient number for full, but orderly discussion. Let every man who fights or pays, exercise his just and equal right in their election. Submit them to approbation or rejection at short intervals. Let the executive be chosen in the same way, and for the same term, by those whose agent he is to be; and leave no screen of a council behind which to skulk from responsibility. It has been thought that the people are not competent electors of judges *learned in the law*. But I do not know that this is true, and, if doubtful, we should follow principle. In this, as in many other elections, they would be guided by reputation, which would not err oftener, perhaps, than the present mode of appointment. In one State of the Union, at least, it has long been tried, and with the most satisfactory success. The judges of

Connecticut have been chosen by the people every six months, for nearly two centuries, and I believe there has hardly ever been an instance of change; so powerful is the curb of incessant responsibility. If prejudice, however, derived from a monarchical institution, is still to prevail against the vital elective principle of our own, and if the existing example among ourselves of periodical election of judges by the people be still mistrusted, let us at least not adopt the evil, and reject the good, of the English precedent; let us retain amovability on the concurrence of the executive and legislative branches, and nomination by the executive alone. Nomination to office is an executive function. To give it to the legislature, as we do, is a violation of the principle of the separation of powers. It swerves the members from correctness, by temptations to intrigue for office themselves, and to a corrupt barter of votes; and destroys responsibility by dividing it among a multitude. By leaving nomination in its proper place, among executive functions, the principle of the distribution of power is preserved, and responsibility weighs with its heaviest force on a single head.

The organization of our county administrations may be thought more difficult. But follow principle, and the knot unties itself. Divide the counties into wards of such size as that every citizen can attend, when called on, and act in person. Ascribe to them the government of their wards in all things relating to themselves exclusively. A justice, chosen by themselves, in each, a constable, a military company, a patrol, a school, the care of their own poor, their own portion of the public roads, the choice of one or more jurors to serve in some court, and the delivery, within their own wards, of their own votes for all elective officers of higher sphere, will relieve the county administration of nearly all its business, will have it better done, and by making every citizen an acting member of the government, and in the offices nearest and most interesting to him, will attach him by his strongest feelings to the independence of his country, and its republican constitution. The justices thus chosen by every ward, would constitute the county court, would do its judiciary business, direct roads and bridges, levy county and poor rates, and administer all the matters of common interest to the whole country. These wards, called townships in New England, are the vital principle of their governments, and have proved themselves the wisest invention ever devised by the wit of man for the perfect exercise of self-government, and for its preservation. We should thus marshal our government into, 1, the general federal republic, for all concerns foreign and federal; 2, that of the State, for what relates to our own citizens exclusively; 3, the county republics, for the duties and concerns of the county; and 4, the ward republics, for the small, and yet numerous and interesting concerns of the neighborhood; and in government, as well as in every other business of life, it is by division and subdivision of duties alone, that all matters, great and small, can be managed to perfection. And the whole is cemented by giving to every citizen, personally, a part in the administration of the public affairs.

The sum of these amendments is, 1. General Suffrage. 2. Equal representation in the legislature. 3. An executive chosen by the people. 4. Judges elective or amovable. 5. Justices, jurors, and sheriffs elective. 6. Ward divisions. And 7. Periodical amendments of the constitution.

I have thrown out these as loose heads of amendment, for consideration and correction; and their object is to secure self-government by the republicanism of our constitution, as well as by the spirit of the people; and to nourish and perpetuate that spirit. I am not among those who fear the people. They, and not the rich, are our dependence for continued freedom. And to preserve their independence, we must not let our rulers load us with perpetual debt. We must make our election between *economy and liberty*, or *profusion and servitude*. If we run into such debts, as that we must be taxed in our meat and in our drink, in our necessaries and our comforts, in our labors and our amusements, for our callings and our creeds, as the people of England are, our people, like them, must come to labor sixteen hours in the twenty-four, give the earnings of fifteen of these to the government for their debts and daily expenses; and the sixteenth being insufficient to afford us bread, we must live, as they now do, on oatmeal and potatoes; have no time to think, no means of calling the mismanagers to account;

but be glad to obtain subsistence by hiring ourselves to rivet their chains on the necks of our fellow-sufferers. Our landholders, too, like theirs, retaining indeed the title and stewardship of estates called theirs, but held really in trust for the treasury, must wander, like theirs, in foreign countries, and be contented with penury, obscurity, exile, and the glory of the nation. This example reads to us the salutary lesson, that private fortunes are destroyed by public as well as by private extravagance. And this is the tendency of all human governments. A departure from principle in one instance becomes a precedent for a second; that second for a third; and so on, till the bulk of the society is reduced to be mere automatons of misery, and to have no sensibilities left but for sinning and suffering. Then begins, indeed, the *bellum omnium in omnia*, which some philosophers observing to be so general in this world, have mistaken it for the natural, instead of the abusive state of man. And the fore horse of this frightful team is public debt. Taxation follows that, and in its train wretchedness and oppression.

Some men look at constitutions with sanctimonious reverence, and deem them like the arc of the covenant, too sacred to be touched. They ascribe to the men of the preceding age a wisdom more than human, and suppose what they did to be beyond amendment. I knew that age well; I belonged to it, and labored with it. It deserved well of its country. It was very like the present, but without the experience of the present; and forty years of experience in government is worth a century of book-reading; and this they would say themselves, were they to rise from the dead. I am certainly not an advocate for frequent and untried changes in laws and constitutions. I think moderate imperfections had better be borne with; because, when once known, we accommodate ourselves to them, and find practical means of correcting their ill effects. But I know also, that laws and institutions must go hand in hand with the progress of the human mind. As that becomes more developed, more enlightened, as new discoveries are made, new truths disclosed, and manners and opinions change with the change of circumstances, institutions must advance also, and keep pace with the times. We might as well require a man to wear still the coat which fitted him when a boy, as civilized society to remain ever under the regimen of their barbarous ancestors. It is this preposterous idea which has lately deluged Europe in blood. Their monarchs, instead of wisely yielding to the gradual change of circumstances, of favoring progressive accommodation to progressive improvement, have clung to old abuses, entrenched themselves behind steady habits, and obliged their subjects to seek through blood and violence rash and ruinous innovations, which, had they been referred to the peaceful deliberations and collected wisdom of the nation, would have been put into acceptable and salutary forms. Let us follow no such examples, nor weakly believe that one generation is not as capable as another of taking care of itself, and of ordering its own affairs. Let us, as our sister States have done, avail ourselves of our reason and experience, to correct the crude essays of our first and unexperienced, although wise, virtuous, and well-meaning councils. And lastly, let us provide in our constitution for its revision at stated periods. What these periods should be, nature herself indicates. By the European tables of mortality, of the adults living at any one moment of time, a majority will be dead in about nineteen years. At the end of that period, then, a new majority is come into place; or, in other words, a new generation. Each generation is as independent as the one preceding, as that was of all which had gone before. It has then, like them, a right to choose for itself the form of government it believes most promotive of its own happiness; consequently, to accommodate to the circumstances in which it finds itself, that received from its predecessors; and it is for the peace and good of mankind, that a solemn opportunity of doing this every nineteen or twenty years, should be provided by the constitution; so that it may be handed on, with periodical repairs, from generation to generation, to the end of time, if anything human can so long endure. It is now forty years since the constitution of Virginia was formed. The same tables inform us, that, within that period, two-thirds of the adults then living are now dead. Have then the remaining third, even if they had the wish, the right to hold in obedience to their will, and to laws heretofore made by them, the other two-thirds, who, with themselves, compose the present mass of adults? If they have not, who has? The dead? But the dead have no rights. They are nothing; and nothing cannot own something. Where there is no substance, there can be no accident. This corporeal globe, and everything upon it, belong to its present corporeal inhabitants, during their generation. They alone have a right to direct what is the concern of themselves alone, and to declare the law of that direction; and this declaration can only be made by their majority. That majority, then, has a right to depute representatives to a convention, and to make the constitution what they think will be the best for themselves. But how collect their voice? This is the real difficulty. If invited by private authority, or county or district meetings, these divisions are so large that few will attend; and their voice will be imperfectly, or falsely pronounced. Here, then, would be one of the advantages of the ward divisions I have proposed. The mayor of every ward, on a question like the present, would call his ward together, take the simple yea or nay of its members, convey these to the county court, who would hand on those of all its wards to the proper general authority; and the voice of the whole people would be thus fairly, fully, and peaceably expressed, discussed, and decided by the common reason of the society. If this avenue be shut to the call of sufferance, it will make itself heard through that of force, and we shall go on, as other nations are doing, in the endless circle of oppression, rebellion, reformation; and oppression, rebellion, reformation, again; and so on forever.

These, Sir, are my opinions of the governments we see among men, and of the principles by which alone we may prevent our own from falling into the same dreadful track. I have given them at greater length than your letter called for. But I cannot say things by halves; and I confide them to your honor, so to use them as to preserve me from the gridiron of the public papers. If you shall approve and enforce them, as you have done that of equal representation, they may do some good. If not, keep them to yourself as the effusions of withered age and useless time. I shall, with not the less truth, assure you of my great respect and consideration.

ABOUT THE AUTHOR

Charles F. Stamper is a husband, father of one, and brother of four. He has worked as a systems analyst, production manager, and in manufacturing for various Fortune 500 corporations. He is the author of The *Grand Old Party*, *The Party of the People*, and now *A Dimes Difference?: Democrats, Republicans and the US National Debt*. He attended Lee's Jr. College and The University of Kentucky. He works, writes, and lives with his wife and daughter in Georgetown, KY.

www.breathittpublishing.com

Charles F. Stamper

I hope you have enjoyed this book and that you may find it useful in some way. Thank you for spending some of that most valuable of assets, your time, with me and I hope to continue our conversations in the future.

Should you be interested, please visit our web site at: "www.breathittpublishing.com".

As for recommendations we have a few:

First would be the following title:

The Constitution of the United States of America,

with all of the Amendments; The Declaration of Independence;

And The Articles of Confederation

ISBN 1449925324   **ISBN-13** 978-1449925321

Secondly, and for a far less serious treatment of the subject:

For having a little fun with your Democratic friends;

The Party of the People:

Everything Right with the Democratic Party in the 21st Century

ISBN-10: 1463778872 **ISBN-13:** 978-1463778873

And lest we not forget your Republican friends;

The Grand Old Party

Everything Right with the Republican Party in the 21st Century

ISBN-13: 978-1463782115 **ISBN-10:** 146378211X

By way of showing our appreciation the following code may be used when checking out for a 10% discount on any of the above titles, or additional copies of this one, when purchased at our site , quantities unlimited.

"WX4LF6PY "

All of our titles are also available at Amazon, in print as well as Kindle versions, or by all means ask your local book store to carry them, or your local library to add them to their collection.

Charles F. Stamper